The Place

of

Humanity

in

GOD'S PURPOSE

John H. Essex

BIBLE STUDENT'S PRESS™

Windber, Pennsylvania

A Facsimile Project

A facsimile reprint is a photographic duplicate of the original work. We dedicate a large amount of time and resources to acquire and preserve original material, the age and condition of which have a direct effect on the outcome of our reproductions. Like the books on which we base our reprints, our copies may contain imperfections such as printing errors and flaws, as well as user markings, notations and underlining. However, we believe that these works are important enough to make available as part of our dedication in protecting, preserving and promoting valuable historical Scripture study resources. Perhaps not unlike many of the books that we re-typeset, we may not always be in full agreement with their contents.

The Place of Humanity in God's Purpose
by John H. Essex (1907-1991)

Facsimile Edition

Nathan H. Pilkington
Facsimile Publication Director

ISBN: 978-1-62904-163-6

Published by
   Bible Student's Press
   An imprint of *Pilkington & Sons*
   P.O. Box 265
   Windber, PA 15963

For information on other Bible study resources,
   www.StudyShelf.com

Printed in the United States of America

THE PLACE OF HUMANITY
IN GOD'S PURPOSE

EXPLANATORY NOTES

WHAT IS MAN?

GOD said, "Let us make man [humanity] in Our image, and according to Our likeness." And God created man [humanity] in His image.

But men have said that humanity has come into being from insignificant beginnings, through a long process of evolution, and have claimed that both men and apes had the same forbears.

WHAT IS MAN?

We propose to discard without delay all the theories of men, and concentrate solely upon the Word of God; but we opened as we did in order to focus attention on the fact that our question has been engaging human minds over the years, with results that are often at variance with Scripture, and completely dishonoring to God. Can we have a greater contrast? On the one hand, created in the image of God. On the other, evolved through the forbears of apes.

What, then, is man? Why was he created? And what is his function in God's great scheme and purpose? Why was he specifically created in God's own image and likeness? Above all, why does he suffer and die?

These are perfectly proper questions to ask, and we hope to give answers that are completely satisfying because they are in full accord with God's Word, and are therefore glorifying to God Himself.

The question is asked several times in the Scriptures. Job asks it in Job 7:17, "What is man, that Thou

shouldest magnify him? And that Thou shouldest set
Thine heart upon him? And that Thou shouldest visit
him every morning, and try him every moment?"

Job was a man passing through affliction, and he is
asking why God should trouble Himself with men, whose
days are numbered in any case. Why cannot God leave
them to pass their few days in peace? Why must He
subject them to such distress?

David asks the question in Psalm 144:3. "Lord, what
is man, that Thou art acknowledging him? Or the son
of a mortal that Thou art reckoning with him? Man is
like to vanity; his days are as a passing shadow."
Apparently, there is nothing of any permanence or con-
sequence in man that God should take such particular
notice of him.

David again asks the question in Psalm 8:3, and here
he sets it against a background of God's most expansive
creations. "For I am seeing Thy heavens, the work of
Thy fingers, the moon and the stars which Thou hast
established. What is a mortal that Thou art mindful of
him? And a son of humanity, that Thou art noting
him?"

Here the psalmist, who in another place cries, "The
heavens declare the glory of God," looks up into these
same heavens, considers their magnitude, and then asks,
"What is man?"—"What is a mortal?"

And when we compare God's terrestrial creation with
His celestial ones, we may well ask, "Why has God
created man?"

*   *   *

At the very beginning of God's Word, we read that He
created the heavens and the earth. This has been ac-
cepted, by those who believe the Scriptures, as a simple
statement of fact, but really it is a very profound truth
indeed. For one thing, have we really considered its
incongruity? It is like saying, God created the ocean

and a raindrop, or God created a continent and a grain of sand. So vast are the heavens; so small is the earth!

We will not take up space in trying to describe the magnitude of the heavens, but let one illustration suffice. There is a well-known constellation of stars known as the Great Bear (Ursa Major). There are many stars in this group, but seven are very prominent, and can be easily seen on any starlit night, for in the northern hemisphere they are clearly visible to the naked eye all the year round. Four of the stars are roughly in the form of a square, with the other three forming a kind of tail (or handle, if you think of the constellation as the Dipper or the Plough, by which names it is also sometimes known).

Now the last star but one in the tail is called Mizar. Near to it is a tiny star (Alcor) which is much fainter than Mizar, but we can ignore this, and just concentrate on Mizar alone. For Mizar itself is a double star—that is, two stars that to the naked eye appear as one. Yet the two components of Mizar are 25 million miles apart, but they are so far away that they appear as one.

It takes just over one second for light to travel from the moon to the earth; it takes rather more than eight minutes for light to travel from the sun to the earth, about 93 million miles. It takes more than 73 *years* for Mizar's light to reach this earth. Or, to put it another way, if the moon were to be darkened, men would know about it in less than two seconds; if the sun were to be darkened, they would know it in under ten minutes, but if Mizar were to lose its light, it would be more than 70 years before any of us would learn about it. And even this is only a small distance in the universe. The light from some of the objects that can be seen in the sky on a cloudless night has been on its way to us since before Adam came into being.

In drawing attention to the vastness of the heavens in contrast to the smallness of the earth, we are doing no more than is done by the Scriptures, when they speak of the inhabitants of the earth as grasshoppers, and whole nations as a drop from a bucket, and as the small fine dust of the balances which no one bothers to blow away because it has so little effect on the measurement. Indeed, Isaiah 40:17 tells us that "all the nations are as nothing in front of Him." When we consider the great upheavals that have been caused by the various eruptions of nations in our own lifetimes, it is especially comforting to be assured that the great God of the universe is completely unmoved by them. They do not affect His purpose any more than does an extra drop in a bucketful of water, or a speck of dust on a pair of scales.

Then "What is a mortal, that Thou art mindful of him?"

"For I am seeing Thy heavens, the work of Thy fingers, the moon and stars which Thou hast established..." It is stated in Scripture that the stars of heaven cannot be numbered by mankind, and this is borne out by astronomy. Every new telescope that is made brings millions of fresh stars, and even new galaxies of stars, into view, so that the mind boggles when trying to assess their numbers. But if it is true that the physical, material content of the heavens is so much greater than that of the earth, what are we to say about the animate spiritual content? Scientists make feeble endeavors to find out whether there is life on the neighboring planets; this is as far as they can go, for they can only think in terms of life as they understand it on this earth. But we are convinced that the universe is full of life—spirit beings with far greater powers than anything possessed by humans, and numerous beyond computation.

Let us note what Nehemiah has to say (Neh. 9:6), "Thou, even Thou, art Lord alone; Thou hast made heaven, the heaven of heavens, with all their host, the earth and all things that are therein, the seas and all that is therein, and Thou preservest them all; *and the host of heaven worshippeth Thee.*" Nehemiah can ignore all the multitudes of earth in this picture; it is the host of heaven that is so important.

But now let us draw attention to one or two points which have been passed over by many believers, and treated too lightly even by many of those who are aware that God's purpose is an eonian one, to be achieved in five eons.

The first point is, that *in the first eon* humanity was not even in existence. Adam was not created until the sixth day of the *second eon.* During the whole of that first eon (and we are not told its length) God's dealings were with other beings, celestial creations. In fact, we can go so far as to say that the heavens were created first, and the earth later, for there were already celestial beings in existence when the foundations of the earth were laid. Hence, Job tells us that when this happened, "the morning stars sang together, and all the sons of God shouted together for joy" (Job 38:7). There must have been some reason for such great jubilation among celestial beings when they saw the earth brought into being; and there must also have been some reason why some of their number, led by the Adversary, brought about the circumstances (whatever they may have been) that led to the disruption of that same earth at the end of that first eon.

That there has been a violent disruption of the earth there can be no doubt. Quite apart from indications in the structure of the earth itself, which indicate a violent upheaval at some time, there are the evidences of Scripture. The Greek word *katabolê*, used ten times in connection with the world, and erroneously translated foundation in the King James (Authorized) Version, literally means down-casting. Notice how the verbal form of the word is used in 2 Corinthians 4:9, "Persecuted but not forsaken, *cast down* but not perishing."

But perhaps the most potent scriptural evidence for the disruption occurs in Genesis 1:2, where we perceive a great contrast from the happenings of verse 1. Let us read the two verses together from the Concordant Translation.

Verse 1: "Created by the Alueim were the heavens and the earth."

Verse 2: "Yet the earth became a chaos and vacant, and darkness was on the surface of the submerged chaos."

In this corrected translation, we see that the first sentence summarizes the orderly process of creation; the second sentence brings in disorder and chaos. God did not create the earth a chaos; He created it to be inhabited (Isa. 45:18). He did not create it in darkness, or out of darkness, as is popularly supposed. He created it in light, for He is light, and darkness in Him there is none (1 John 1:5). Darkness comes when light is withdrawn, and, in Scripture is associated with the Adversary (Satan) (Eph. 6:11, 12), and here (in Gen. 1:2) we see a first reference to that jurisdiction of darkness later spoken of by both Jesus and Paul (Luke 22:53; Col. 1:13).

Consideration of these and other scriptures leads us to the conclusion that there must have been a rebellion against God during that first eon, which ended with the disruption of the world and the imposition of darkness. This rebellion must have been among the hosts of heaven, for humanity was not yet in existence. Man was not responsible for the earth becoming a chaos and vacant, nor for the darkness which came with it, for man was not yet created. Nor was man primarily the cause of the slaying of the Lambkin, for, in Revelation 13:8, we read of "the Lambkin *slain from the disruption of the world*," and again we emphasize that humanity was not in existence at the disruption.

In Ephesians 6:11, Paul says, "Put on the panoply of God, to enable you to stand up to the stratagems of the

Adversary, for it is not ours to wrestle with blood and flesh, but with the sovereignties, with the authorities, with the world-mights of this darkness, with the *spiritual forces of wickedness among the celestials.*" Humans are foolish to quarrel among themselves, for the real enemies of God's purpose are those immensely powerful spiritual forces of wickedness among the celestials, who have consistently opposed God's purpose wherever it has been revealed, and who caused such havoc in that first eon as to bring about the chaos and darkness that subsequently ensued.

What we are suggesting is that humanity was not the cause of all evil, but rather a rectifying, remedial factor —a special creation, an entirely new order of beings, brought in to correct the evil wrought by Satan among the original celestial creations of God. This is not to suggest that humanity has the power to rectify matters, for, as we shall hope to show later, humanity (like all creation) was made subject to vanity in order that, of itself, it might achieve nothing. No, we are not suggesting that men can reconcile the universe to God, but, rather, that God Himself can achieve this stupendous thing by using "the *form* of humanity"—the form of that special creation which He has created for this very purpose. (See Rom. 8:3; Phil. 2:8).

For we are convinced, after much consideration of the matter, that what occurred in that first eon, before the disruption of the world, was nothing less than a direct challenge by the Adversary to the headship of Christ by stirring up rebellion among celestial beings, by drawing many away from their loyalty to God and His Son, and by thus creating an estrangement between them and God —an estrangement which they had no means of rectifying. Sooner or later, it seems, many would perceive this. The morning stars and the sons of God are evidently those elements that retained their loyalty to God, but they could see no way out of the impasse until the

foundations of the earth were laid. Then they burst
into applause. How much they knew of God's intentions
we cannot say, but evidently they sensed here *a new
development in God's purpose*, which offered them an
assurance for the future. Hence they sang together
and shouted for joy.

And, again, taking a long step forward, may we suggest that when that Saviour was announced, Whose subsequent death was to reconcile all in heaven and earth
to God—when His birth as a child of humanity was
publicly proclaimed by a single messenger (possibly
Gabriel) to the shepherds, those same loyal elements
among the celestials immediately, suddenly, burst into
spontaneous praise to God, for in this Son of Mankind
they saw the divine answer to all the problems that beset
them as celestials, and for which they could find no
answer among themselves.

Are we being fanciful in our suppositions? Well, let
us go back to Psalm 8. Beginning at verse 4, David
asks, "What is a mortal, that Thou art mindful of him?
And the son of humanity that Thou art noting him?"
He then continues, "Yet *lacking little* art Thou making
him *of the messengers* [LXX], and with glory and honor
art Thou crowning him." What a peculiar statement!
(The AV reads: Thou hast made him a little lower than
the angels.) Yet in this statement there seems to be a
first clue to the real answer to the question, "What is
man?"

In the remainder of the Psalm, David speaks of the
dominion which was given to mankind, for he says, "All
dost Thou set under his feet," and then goes on to
elaborate the statement, "Flocks and domestic animals,
all of them, and even the beasts of the field; the birds
of the heavens and the fish of the sea." This is the
dominion originally given to mankind in Adam (Gen.
1:28).

Now let us see how the writer of Hebrews makes use

of this passage. In Hebrews 2:6, we read, "What is man, that Thou are mindful of him? Or a son of mankind that Thou art visiting him? *Thou makest him some bit inferior to messengers*, with glory and honor Thou wreathest him, and dost place him over the works of Thy hands. All dost Thou subject under his feet."

Up to here, allowing for differences of translation, this is a direct and exact quotation from the psalm. David went on to define that which was made subject to man, namely domestic animals, beasts of the field, birds, and fish. The writer of Hebrews omits this definition, for he wants to stress a different point. He presses home the *total* nature of that subjection. *All* was to be subject to man; nothing was to be left unsubject to him. "Yet," he continues, "now we are not as yet seeing all subject to him." From the moment that man allowed a serpent to rule his conduct, he lost his authority over the lower creatures. This was the insidious nature of the Adversary's attack on Adam—challenging his headship over the lower creatures by appearing in the guise of one of them and seducing his complement—woman.

But now the writer of Hebrews takes hold of this passage from the psalm, and gives it a special application (verses 9, 10). "What is man?" was the question, "that Thou art mindful of him?" "Yet we are observing Jesus, Who has been made some bit inferior to messengers—" Here the generic term man is abandoned in favor of the specific name Jesus, thus indicating that, when man was created, it was with an ultimate objective in mind—an objective which would be accomplished by Jesus in the likeness of humanity. And the writer continues by inserting something that was not in the psalm at all, yet which gives the key to the whole matter; "We are observing Jesus, Who has been made some bit inferior to messengers, *because of the suffering of death*, wreathed with glory and honor, so that He should, in the grace of God, *be tasting death for everyone*."

Humanity, it would appear, came into being because of the sufferings of death. Celestials, as such, do not die (Luke 20:36), and the creation of an inferior order of beings was necessary in order that the Son of God Himself could partake of the sufferings of death, and thus for all time settle the question of sin. By coming in fashion as a human (Phil. 2:8), He could offer Himself in a manner acceptable to God and through the sufferings represented by "the blood of His cross," bring back to God all in heaven as well as all on earth.

Now can we see the answer to our question, "What is man?" We are suggesting that humanity was created to be the vehicle in which the Lord Jesus could come in order to become obedient unto death, even the death of the cross, so that He might be the means of reconciling not merely all on earth but all in the heavens also. This text, Colossians 1:20, is conclusive proof, if any is needed, that there is still enmity and estrangement to God in the heavens as well as on this earth.

We are therefore submitting to you that, when we read in the very first chapter of Genesis, "It is becoming light," we are seeing the first signs of the dispersal of that deep spiritual darkness which surrounded the celestials as a result of their rebellion against God in that first eon, and of which the physical darkness that engulfed the earth was merely a sign and a token. And when we read down that first chapter of Genesis and see the restoration of the earth after the chaos caused by the disruption, when it became a chaos and vacant— when we read of vegetation reappearing and of animal life being created, we are, in fact, seeing the stage being set for Golgotha. The props are being prepared!

All the three kingdoms were required to effect the events surrounding the crucifixion. The vegetable kingdom was represented by the wood of the cross, and by the crown of thorns; the mineral kingdom by the nails which pierced the Victim's hands and feet; the animal kingdom by the thongs which lacerated His back. (The animal kingdom also provided all the typical sacrifices which, throughout the centuries, pointed to the real Sacrifice). Only the human element was missing, and this had to be a special creation, made in the image and likeness of God, in order that He, Who was His true Image and Likeness, might come in human form without ever losing that resemblance to God.

Here is the glory and honor with which man is wreathed—being created in the image and likeness of God, in order that God's objective might ultimately be achieved through One in the likeness of humanity. This One would suffer death for the universe, and so remove, once and for all, the cause of all estrangement from God. The irony in the creation of humanity lies in this, that events were to prove that man himself could not provide the Saviour, only His murderers. The Sacrifice was to be provided by God alone (see Gen. 22:8), yet humanity, in the person of a single woman, was graciously permitted to bring forth the One in Whom that Sacrifice should come.

It is to be noted that six times in the first chapter of Genesis, (namely, in verses 4, 10, 12, 18, 21, and 25), God looks at what has been accomplished and declares it to be "good." But after the creation of humanity, and the asserting of man's dominion over the rest, He looks at all that He has made and pronounces it to be "very good" (verse 31). Yes, very good for the purpose for which all was designed, for at this point, God ceases from all the work that He has made, secure in the knowledge that He has implanted within it the impetus that will carry it straight through to the fulfillment (but no more) of everything that He has purposed in it.

* * *

It has been said that the earth is the theater of the universe—that the earth is a stage, on which all the main events of God's purpose are being enacted, watched by a vast audience in the auditorium of the heavens. This may well be true, but we also believe that the earth is an operating theater as well as a display theater. These words are being written close to a great city, in which there are many hospitals. Each of these has a special room, an operating theater, where cases of serious illness are brought for surgery. Also in this same city are several cemeteries. The purpose of the operating theaters is to keep people out of the cemeteries as long as possible.

Now, in the whole universe of God there is only one operating theater and one cemetery. The earth is both, and the remarkable fact is that the one major operation that has been performed in the theater had the immediate result of putting a Man into a cemetery. It is an essential feature of Paul's evangel that Christ not only died but was also entombed before being roused from among the dead. It is also a fact that, of all the many millions of tombs in this vast cemetery called earth, only one is of special significance, and that because it housed for a short while the crucified Lord of glory.

Peter told his hearers on the day of Pentecost that *Jesus* was given up "in the specific counsel and foreknowledge of God." Paul, in Romans 8, speaks of God, "Who spares not His own Son, but gives Him up for us all." It was God, then, Who performed this operation, holding the knife over His own Son, even as in figure Abraham held the knife over Isaac. And was the operation successful, even though it put a Man straight into a tomb? Humanity would declare at once that it was a failure. But God, through His apostle Paul, declares that the evangel, which preaches the word of the cross, is indeed God's power for salvation, and that the blood of Christ's cross brings individual peace and reconciles all, whether on earth or in heaven, to God. And the emptying of the one tomb will eventually result in the

emptying of all the rest, so that the earth will no longer
be a cemetery at all.

> Sing, O sing with exultation,
> Let the joyful tidings spread.
> Herald wide the proclamation,
> Christ is risen from the dead!
>
> All the bonds of death are riven,
> All its doors are opened wide.
> Back the grave its prize has given,
> Yielding up the Crucified!
>
> Christ is risen, He has broken
> All the power of death and sin.
> He, the Firstfruit, is the Token
> Till the rest is gathered in.

THE VANITY OF HUMAN ENDEAVOR

"THE WORDS of the Assembler, a son of David, a king of Israel, in Jerusalem. Vanity of vanities! says the Assembler. Vanity of vanities! The whole is vain."

These are the opening words of Ecclesiastes (CV), and are followed by the phrase, "What advantage has a man in all his toil, with which he is toiling under the sun?"

They occur again at the end of the book, where we read (12:6 AV), "Or ever the silver cord be loosed, or the golden bowl be broken, or the pitcher be broken at the fountain, or the wheel broken at the cistern. Then shall the dust return to the earth as it was: and the spirit shall return unto God Who gave it. Vanity of vanities, saith the Preacher, all is vanity."

What the Assembler is saying is, that despite all the sum total of human endeavor, there is no advantage in it beyond the grave. For, subject as it is to the slavery of corruption, it is therefore deficient in the vitality that would ensure its perpetuity.

In the words of the hymn writer,

> How vain is all beneath the skies!
>   How transient every earthly bliss!
> How slender all the fondest ties
>   That bind us to a world like this!

Is this a true assessment of the position? If so, what is the place of humanity in God's purpose?

The book of Ecclesiastes immediately follows the Book of Rules, commonly called Proverbs, which has, as its declared aims, "For the knowledge of wisdom and admonition, for understanding sayings of understanding, for taking intelligent admonition, justice and judgment and equities, for giving craft to simpletons, to youth knowledge and planning." This book contains much splendid advice as to how men should live, such as,

"The fear of Jehovah is the beginning of knowledge" (1:7).

"Kindness and truth must not forsake you" (3:3).

"Trust in Jehovah with all your heart, and lean not on your own understanding. In all your ways acknowledge Him, then *He* will straighten your paths" (3:5, 6).

But this Book of Rules, with all its good advice—with all its encouragement towards good and wise living—is followed by Ecclesiastes, which concludes everything under the heading of vanity. This word occurs nearly forty times in the book, and is repeated five times in the opening passage for the sake of emphasis. "Vanity of vanities" means "utter vanity."

It does not matter at which aspect of human life we look, it comes to the same end, and is reduced to the same level of nothingness, when death overtakes it. Ecclesiastes examines many of these aspects in turn, and, at the end, sums up the position in these words (12:13, 14 AV):

"Let us hear the conclusion of the whole matter: Fear God and keep His commandments; for this is the whole duty of man. For God shall bring every work into judgment, with every secret thing, whether it be good or whether it be evil."

What a message with which to end a book! If all that God can tell us is that He is going to bring every work of ours into judgment, then we are going to be very wretched indeed. We are going to be like Paul in Romans 7:18-24, where he describes himself,

"For I am aware that good is not making its home in me (that is, in my flesh), for to will is lying beside me, yet to be effecting the ideal is not. For it is not the good that I will that I am doing, but the evil that I am not willing, this I am putting into practice. Now if what I am not willing, this *I* am doing, it is no longer *I* who am effecting it, but Sin which is making its home in me.

"Consequently, I am finding the law that, at my willing to be doing the ideal, the evil is lying beside me. For I am gratified with the law of God as to the man within, yet I am observing a different law in my members warring with the law of my mind, and leading me into captivity to the law of sin which is in my members. "A wretched man am I! What will rescue me out of this body of death?"

We leave the answer to that question for the moment, while we look at a different scripture.

THE CLOUD OF WITNESSES

The eleventh chapter of the epistle to the Hebrews deals wholly with the subject of faith, and lists a long series of individuals who were commended for their exercise of faith. Then why should we write about "vanity"? Would we not be better employed in considering the subject of faith?

We wonder how many people, reading down this chapter, are aware that the list of faithful characters is headed by Abel whose name means "Vanity," and that he, though long since dead, is still speaking! Why is Abel (Vanity) still speaking, and what, in fact, is he saying? We note, in passing, that he has been dead longer than any other man!

In the preceding article of our series, we suggested that humanity was created in order to correct something that had gone awry in a higher sphere. A whole eon had elapsed before humanity was brought into being—

an eon which saw the creation of the heavens and the
earth, the "then world" or system (*kosmos*) that per-
ished (2 Pet. 3:6)—an eon which began in light and
concluded in darkness and chaos. Such disruption must
be seen in the light of God's purpose.

We remind ourselves again that the Lambkin was
"slain from the disruption of the world" (Rev. 13:8).
Clearly, God regarded the Lambkin as being slain before
ever man came into being; therefore Adam's sin was not
the first cause of the sacrifice of Christ. It was among
the celestials that the original disturbance took place
that necessitated the slaying of the Lambkin; in fact,
this became inevitable from the moment that an Adversary
was created (Job 26:13). Satan himself was a celestial being, and would, before the creation of humanity, undoubtedly seek to oppose God by sowing seeds of rebellion among
his fellow celestials, who, numerous and powerful though
they might be, had no means in themselves of remedying the position—of removing the enmity and estrangement—of rectifying the damage caused by Satan's acti-
vities among them.

Hence humanity was created as a special and separate
order of beings, specifically made in the image and
likeness of God, in order that God's own Son, the Highest in the universe, and indeed its Head, might empty
Himself to come in the form of humanity, yet *without
losing His likeness to God*. Then He might humble
Himself to become obedient unto death, even the death
of the cross, thus providing the means by which sin
(missing the mark) should be for all time effectively put
out of the way, and consequently enmity effaced. Complete reconciliation of all in heaven, as well as on earth,
is the ultimate effect of the peace made through the
blood of Christ's cross.

(To anticipate a later part of this study, we may add
that this special creation, humanity, also becomes the
channel through which the ecclesia, the body of Christ,

would be called upon to pass that it, too, might share the enmity and estrangement of creation so that it might ultimately be saved in grace, and be used of God to display to the celestials the "transcendent riches of His grace" (Eph. 2:7). The kindness which God has shown to us, sinners and enemies though we were, will be the criterion, the evidence, the proof of His intention to shower His grace upon those erring ones of that first eon.)

Thus we see that humanity was specially created in the image and likeness of God in order to be the vehicle through which the whole universe will ultimately be reconciled to Him. But, in saying this, let us ever remember that humanity is only the instrument in the hands of God, and never the guiding hand or the driving force. The glory of decision and the glory of operation both belong to God alone; this glory He will never give to another. Even God's Son could only do the works which His God and Father gave Him to do.

But this special creation, humanity, was not unnoticed by the Adversary. He was soon on the scene, as he always is wherever there is a special development in God's purpose, and we know how he deceived humanity by seducing the weaker part. It is an interesting point that there is no record of Satan attacking humanity until it was divided and he could attack one part while the other was absent.

The Adversary succeeded in getting Adam branded as a sinner. As a sinner, deserving of God's indignation, he is displayed to the whole universe. What must the celestials have thought? Man, this exceptional creation of God, succumbing to the Adversary's attack and expelled from the garden in which he had been placed, and (terrible beyond measure!) made subject to death— something never previously even thought of. What hope could there be?

But there was hope still, and that hope lay in the

promise made to the woman that her seed should bruise the serpent's head. Soon a son was born to her. She was delighted; what woman would not be? This was the first son ever born, and she called him Cain, which means "Acquired." "I have acquired a man, Jehovah," she said. Here, she probably thought, is the promised seed. Here is the one who would rectify her transgression. Here is the one who would bruise the serpent's head.

But if Eve really thought this, she must soon have become disillusioned. The workings of death may have become apparent in her offspring, or perhaps she was taught the vanity of human endeavor by her husband. Whichever way it was, when her second son came along she called him Abel (Vanity). Her longing was in vain. The seed that should fulfill God's intention could never come from Adam.

And Abel himself, by the offering which he made to God from the firstlings of his flock, gave witness to the same great truth. Abel believed what he had obviously learned of God, for we are told that it was by faith that he made this offering. Equally certain, Cain did not believe God but thought he could do better by offering the toil of his own hands. His offering was unacceptable, but instead of remedying the matter by doing as Abel had done, he was either too proud or too obstinate, became angry, and slew his brother.

Abel has been dead longer than any other man. As far as we know, he was the first to die. He died long before Adam. Perhaps more than any other, his death proclaims the futility of human endeavor, for all that Cain achieved was the destruction of his brother.

The way of Cain has become the way of humanity as a whole. It is opposed to the way of God. It is the product of human thought and human action. It is a way which began with the murder of a just Abel, and reached its peak of infamy in the murder of a greater than Abel, the righteous Son of God.

THE LESSON OF VANITY

The efforts of men, when not directed and governed by the Spirit of God, invariably lead to vanity. This is a truth that has to be learned by every generation of humanity, and is still not learned by humanity as a whole.

Abraham had to learn it, too. He was promised a son, but time went by, and the promise remained unfulfilled. He thought he could perhaps help God by expediting matters, and Ishmael was born. But Ishmael was not the promised seed and only became an obstacle in Abraham's relationship with God, so that eventually he had to be sent away. God does not need human help; He is all-sufficient in Himself, and Isaac, the promised seed, came in God's own due time.

David had to learn the lesson. In the power of God, he could slay Goliath; yet in his own strength, he could fall to the charms of a woman and seriously compromise his own future and the honor of the nation he had been chosen to lead. Subsequently David saw his folly and repented, but he could not undo what had been done.

Peter had to learn the lesson. In the presence of Jesus, he could be exceedingly bold, but when the power of Jesus was temporarily slackened, he could deny Him three times. When the lesson came home, Peter wept bitterly.

Paul had to learn the lesson. In his own strength, he persecuted the ecclesia and wasted it. He was stopped suddenly before he could widen the range of his persecution. Afterwards he included his former zeal among the things which he counted as refuse that he might win Christ.

But what are we to say about the acts of all those mentioned in Hebrews eleven? Are not these men and women being commended for what they did? How then can we speak of all human endeavor as being in vain? Surely some of the things we do are useful and helpful?

Let us remind ourselves that this list is headed by a
man whose name was Vanity. It is significant that this
very name stands at the head of the list.

If we examine the acts of those mentioned here, we
shall find that invariably they are commended, not for
things which they do of their own initiative, but solely
for acts undertaken in accord with, and under the
direction of, their faith in God. In effect, it is their
faith that is being commended.

For example, Abraham is being commended for his
long journey at God's behest from his former home in Ur
of the Chaldees to the land of Canaan, but he is not
commended for his subsequent journey into Egypt,
which he took of his own volition in order to escape the
famine which he found prevailing in Canaan when he
arrived. Abraham did not realize that when God gave
him the land He gave him the famine with it. Abraham
should have stayed where he was and trusted in God to
provide. Instead he did (as probably we all would have
done in similar circumstances) what he thought was
best; but he immediately involved himself in difficulties
which needed the intervention of the Lord to extricate
him.

Again, Moses was not commended for his striking of
the Egyptian, nor for his later striking of the rock, but
for his disassociating himself with the lures and riches
of Egypt, preferring to suffer with his people rather than
to enjoy the pleasures of sin, which could have been his
through continued residence in Egypt.

Rahab is not commended for being a prostitute, but
for the way in which she protected the respresentatives
of the people of God.

But perhaps the most striking example is that of
Abraham again, coupled also with Isaac and Jacob, that
they dwelt in the land of promise for so long and never
built themselves permanent dwellings. Abraham had
come from a cultured city, Ur of the Chaldees; the

people around him in the new land dwelt in cities like Sodom and Gomorrah, yet though Abraham lived exactly 100 years from the date of his entry into the land, he never built himself a house, but remained a nomad. "For he waited for a city having foundations, whose Artificer and Architect is God" (Heb. 11:10). Thus we see that Abraham is commended for something that he did *not* do.

The people of Israel today, in the same land that Abraham received from God, are building themselves cities—not waiting for that holy city which God will prepare for them and which one of their apostles, John, was permitted to see in a vision.

As we have seen before, humanity was specially created in the likeness of God's Image to be the vehicle through which the reconciliation of the universe was to be effected; and yet, after somewhere around two thousand years, it was all but completely wiped out, so sinful had it become. Only one family, that of Noah, was spared to carry the race forward. So much, indeed, for human effort!

And after a few more centuries, the pride of human endeavor sought to raise itself again, and God scattered humanity as it sought to build a tower rising to heaven that it might achieve itself a name.

Israel, the descendants of Abraham, whom God had specially chosen to be His own people, were actually committing idolatry even while the law was being given to their leader, Moses. Eventually, after many judgments had fallen upon them because of repeated idolatries, they were scattered to all quarters of the earth, and their capital, Jerusalem, was destroyed. Where is all this leading?

Moses, great prophet though he was, had to point to a *Greater Prophet*, whom the Lord, the God of Israel, would raise up. The priesthood of Aaron would have to give way to a greater priesthood, that according to the order of Melchizedek, of whom it was written that he was "fatherless, motherless, without a genealogy" (Heb. 7:3)—in other words, no human connections are tied to the Melchizedek priesthood, otherwise it would be no different from the former.

The kings Saul, David, and Solomon, each ruled forty years over a united kingdom, but each fell short of God's requirements, and the kingdom was divided immediately after the death of Solomon. But the prophet Jeremiah was inspired to say that God would raise unto David a righteous Branch, and a King would reign and prosper (23:5).

The prophets, priests and kings of Israel, anointed though they were, could only point forward to greater than themselves; not one could achieve the ideal in himself. Moses, under God's direction, might deliver the people from Egypt, but sin in himself intervened to prevent him from taking them into the promised land. David, in God's strength, might slay Goliath, but he was not permitted to build God's temple.

Now all this would be somber indeed, were it not for the fact that the ineffectiveness of human endeavor cannot nullify either the purpose or the promises of God. It is the apostle Paul who puts the matter into proper perspective for us.

In all his writings, this apostle seems to emphasize two particular words, *one* and *all*. Men try to turn the word *one* into *many*, and the word *all* into *some*.

For instance, men make themselves *many* gods and *many* lords, but Paul knows only *one* God and *one* Lord (1 Cor. 8:6). Men would have *many* faiths, but Paul knows only *one* faith; *many* ecclesias, but Paul knows only *one* ecclesia, that which is the body of Christ; *many* expectations, yet Paul insists on *one* expectation of our calling (*cf* Eph. 4:4, 5). And Paul sees only one Saviour of the universe, and he stresses, in Romans 5:19, that it is through the obedience of the *One* that the many descendants of Adam shall be constituted just.

Men would make the acts of *many* the basis of justification; God, through His apostle, says that it is the obedience of the *One* that counts. That One Man, for Whom the whole human race was created, is Christ Jesus. He is the *One* through Whom the grace of God will superabound to Adam's many descendants (Rom. 5:15).

And so, although the sum total of all the acts of the *many* result in vanity, the acts of the *One* achieve all that God had in mind when He created humanity. But to see in detail how God overcomes the vanity of human endeavor, we must devote a separate study.

THE LESSONS OF THE POTTER

Most of you who read these words will at some time or other have been to an exhibition, for all kinds of shows are held in the main countries of the world every year. Generally they are designed to be instructive and to further the interests of those who are putting on the display. They are often made up of different stands, each presenting its own theme. In a travel exhibition, for example, one stand might portray the grandeur of the United States, another the historical attractions of Britain, another the various means of travel from place to place, another the advantages of being able to converse with peoples of foreign countries. On each stand will be placed the best examples that can be found to illustrate its particular theme, and everything will be done, through arrangement and lighting effects, to enhance its impact.

Now this idea of putting things on exhibition in order to demonstrate certain facts is by no means new and has indeed been used by God on many occasions. For instance, He has filled the heavens with stars in order to display His majesty and glory. "The heavens declare (*or* are rehearsing) the glory of God," says the Psalmist (Psalm 19:1). This is a display that is going on all the time; it was true in David's day, when the psalm was written. It was true back in Abraham's time, for was not he told to gaze into the heavens and count the stars and see if it were possible to number them? It is still true today. It is a tremendous display of God's greatness and wisdom and power, both in the creation and in the control of such a multitude of heavenly bodies, and it is rehearsed for us both by day and by night. "Day unto day uttereth speech, and night unto night showeth knowledge."

And into whatever aspects of creation we look, whether into the infinitely great or the infinitesimally small, we find the majesty of God displayed. Indeed, as Paul reminds us in the beginning of his Roman letter, the achievements of God from the creation of the world have been used by Him to make Himself known to humanity, so that nobody shall have an excuse if he fails to give Him the thanks that are rightly His due. In Him we live and move and are, and everything around us gives testimony to this, so that on this ground alone, without reference to the Scriptures, we should be prepared to acknowledge God as our Creator, Provider and Sustainer.

But to move from the general to the particular, we find one special way in which God chose to display a portrait of Himself, and this was in the person of His Son. "Lord, show us the Father," said Philip to Jesus. Jesus told him, "He who has seen Me has seen the Father" (John 14:8, 9). Christ is truly the Image of the invisible God, and in the person of Jesus all facets of the Father are revealed.

But now let us look at a particular incident in the Hebrew Scriptures, where God invited one of His prophets to observe something which would give God the opportunity to explain to him His intentions concerning His people, Israel. We are thinking of the occasion when Jeremiah visited the potter's house. Let us read from Jeremiah 18:

> The word which comes to Jeremiah from Ieue, saying,
> "Rise and go down to the house of the potter,
> And there I will announce to you My words."
> And I am going down to the house of the potter,
> And behold! He is making a work on the stones (*or* wheels).

Yet the vessel which he is making of the clay
Is ruined in the hand of the potter.
And he turns it back and is making another vessel of it,
As it is upright in the eyes of the potter to make it.
And coming is the word of Ieue to me, saying,
"As this potter does, cannot I do to you, house of Israel?"
   Averring is Ieue,
"Behold! As the clay in a potter's hand,
So are you in My hand, house of Israel.
The moment I speak of a nation or of a kingdom,
To pluck them up, to break down and to destroy,
And that nation turns back
From all their evil, of which I spoke,
Then I regret the evil which I had designed to do to them.
And the moment I speak of a nation or of a kingdom,
To build and to plant,
And they do evil in My eyes,
To avoid hearkening to My voice,
Then I regret the good, the good I spoke to do to them.
And now, speak, pray, to the men of Judah,
And to the dwellers of Jerusalem, saying,
'Thus says Ieue: Behold! I am forming evil against you
  ...'"

In this passage, we have God using a little scene in
a potter's house to illustrate several vital truths—truths
of supreme importance and magnitude—great Divine
priniciples which, though here applied to Israel, nevertheless obtain all through the eons. Here we have a
potter with a vessel in his hands that he has just made,
and he finds a flaw in it, so he immediately crushes it in
his hands and makes it again, another vessel, as it seemed
good to the potter to do so. The lessons that we learn
from this simple exhibition of the potter's craft are
many.

First, *the potter has the power to do what he wills
with that which is in his hand.* Similarly, God has the
power to do whatever He wills with whatever is in His
hand. The house of Israel was in God's hand; they were
His people. "Cannot I do with you as this potter?"
saith the Lord.

Second, the potter has not only the power *but also the*

right to do what he wills with whatever is in his hand.
Paul emphasizes this point when he, in spirit, visits a
similar pottery, for he says in Romans 9:20, 21, "That
which is molded will not protest to the molder, Why do
you make me thus? Or has not the potter the right over
the clay, out of the same kneading to make one vessel,
indeed, for honor, yet one for dishonor?" The right
lies with the potter, not with the clay, and when the
potter finds a flaw in the vessel that is in his hand, he
has the right to destroy it and remake it. And God has
the right to do this with Israel, who has become marred
in His hand.

Third, *the marred vessel never leaves the hand of the
potter.* It is not put on display until it satisfies its
maker as being perfect for the use for which he has designed it. Israel, in spite of all that nation's deficiencies,
has never been out of the Potter's hand. God has always
held her secure.

Fourth, *the potter can destroy as well as create,* and
from this action of the potter, we learn the great truth
that God can create evil as well as good. The prophet
Isaiah tells us that God is the Creator of evil (Isaiah
45:7); the prophet Jeremiah tells us that God, on occasions, forms evil. "Thus saith the Lord, behold I frame
evil against you" (AV). But when *God* does so, it is
always that good may come out of it, as when He
crucified His own Son. But surely *men* crucified the
Lord of glory! Indeed, they did, but they were only
instruments to effect God's purpose. Peter, on the day of
Pentecost, speaks of Jesus as "This One, given up in the
specific counsel and foreknowledge of God" (Acts 2:23).
Later, in his first epistle, he writes of "the precious blood
of Christ, as of a flawless and unspotted lamb, foreknown, indeed, before the disruption of the world"
(1 Pet. 1:19, 20). John, in Revelation 13:8, refers to
"the Lambkin slain from the disruption of the world."

The disruption of the world, as we have noted earlier,

was that event right at the beginning of Genesis, which brought chaos and darkness on the scene, and submerged the original creation in water, before the Spirit of God moved over the face of the waters and brought light to the scene. This was the point at which the Lambkin was slain, and humanity was not then in existence. How could any of the sons of Adam be responsible for this primal decision of God?

Thus, the display in the potter's house gives us the real explanation of evil at the hand of God. It is in order that He may erase all defects so that the ultimate outcome may be to His glory. And now let us note a fifth point. The potter *remakes* the vessel, he does not *repair* it. When God's purpose concerning Israel is accomplished, it will not result in a patched-up job. There will be no concealed defects. And this is true of all of God's creations. When once anything becomes marred, it must be made afresh. God does not say, "Lo! I patch all up," but, "Lo! I make all new."

And, a sixth point, when God makes anew, He does it *as it pleases Him*. The potter makes it again another vessel, as it seems good to the potter to do so. Once, when on holiday, I saw this little scene in the potter's house enacted exactly as Jeremiah describes. It was in a little pottery in South Wales, and over the door were the words of Romans that have already been quoted, only, of course, they were in the more familiar rendering of the Authorized Version, "Hath not the potter power over the clay, of the same lump to make one vessel unto honor, and another unto dishonor?"

As we watched the potter, he had a vase in his hand. Something about it displeased him, for he immediately crushed it, slapped the clay back on the revolving wheel, and his fingers began to fashion a bowl. He exercised his prerogative to make what he pleased with what was in his hand, and it was not the same as before. It might have been; he might have made another vase, but he did not. He made something else, something different. And this opens up a wide field for consideration if we care to explore it, though it is not strictly relevant to the context of Jeremiah, which relates solely to Israel.

If, for example, we look at the new creation in Christ Jesus as the achievement of a Divine hand (as it surely is—we are "God's achievement, being created in Christ Jesus for good works"—Eph. 2:10) then it is certainly not fashioned the same as the old. "The primitive passed by. Lo! there has come new" (2 Cor. 5:17). And the bodies which will be ours in resurrection will not be like these bodies of humiliation which we now possess; they will be conformed to the body of Christ's glory. And the new heavens and the new earth will not be like the old heavens and the old earth which are to be destroyed, for the former will not be remembered nor even brought to mind.

"Arise, and go down to the potter's house, and there I will cause thee to hear My words" (AV).

God is an ideal Instructor, but if we wish to learn of Him we must go to the place to which He directs us. Jeremiah went to the potter's house; we must go to the Scriptures. We shall not find enlightenment concerning God's character and intentions in the philosophies of the world; without exception they teach us that we must seek to make something better out of what already exists, however marred or however imperfect that may be. Some are so optimistic as to preach that we are steadily advancing by a process of evolution from immaturity to perfection, despite evidences on every hand that moral standards are much lower today than they were even a few years ago.

Truly, God's ways are not man's ways, and man's wisdom is stupidity with God, for the simple reason that it consistently ignores the basic principle that God never *mends* but always *remakes*. And when He remakes, He consults nobody else, but does it in a manner that pleases

Him. He operates all in accord with the counsel of His own will.

The lessons to be learned in a potter's house are truly many and varied. The Hebrew word *yahtzar* or *itzr*, translated "potter" in Jeremiah 18, is also translated "form" or "former" in other places, and when we read in Genesis 2:7 that the Lord God (Ieue Alueim) is *forming* the human of soil from the ground, we have a description of the Potter at work. Cannot we see His hands forming—fashioning—a vessel in His own Image and likeness? All humanity is in the hands of the Potter, and if humanity becomes marred in His hands, we have the scriptural assurance of a new humanity, in which there is no marring.

Some years ago, when speaking on this subject, we concluded by remarking that there is only one Potter. To us there is only one God. All is out of Him. A brother then reminded us that there is also only one clay. Yes, all humanity is of the same stock; and of the same kneading God can make one vessel to honor and one to dishonor. That is to say, there is nothing intrinsically different in the makeup of those who are designated vessels of honor and those who are appointed to be vessels of dishonor. The basic ingredient is the same. We are all of the same kneading, of the same clay. Let us always remember this. If we think of ourselves as being chosen of God, it is not because of any virtue in ourselves. Fundamentally we are no different from our fellows; we have nothing within ourselves of which to boast.

In the hands of the potter, the clay is powerless, but in his hands it can be adapted for any use that the potter may determine. And humanity in the hand of God is equally impotent, yet can be used by Him to achieve the purpose for which it was created in His image and likeness. Even the Lord Jesus came to be of the one clay. He came to be in the likeness of

humanity (Phil. 2:7). He was born of a woman and
thus given the form in which He was to minister and do
the will of God. The flesh He wore was the flesh of
humanity. Though Himself without sin, because of the
life He had received direct from His Father, He
nevertheless came in the likeness of sin's flesh that He
might condemn sin in the flesh (Rom. 8:3). In appearance He was like any other man; His flesh was the same
as any other man's flesh, liable to the same inherent
passions and lusts which however in His case were
always kept under complete control by His God-given
Spirit. If this were not so, how could He have been
tested by the Adversary in the way that He was?
Satan tested Him in His weakened state towards the end
of a forty-day fast by appealing to the desires of the
flesh; Jesus withstood the attacks by the exercise of the
powers of His Spirit. In Christ, humanity found its
highest expression; He is the Son of Mankind, but let
us not forget that He is also the Son of God, and in Him
God finds the fulfillment of all that He had in mind
when He created humanity.

Though all the millions of human beings, who are
descended from Adam, can of themselves accomplish
nothing—"all is vanity"—yet God, through the One
Who came in the likeness of humanity and was actually
born of a woman, can accomplish all, and can through
Him reconcile all to Himself, whether in earth or in
heaven (Col. 1:20).

THE POTTER'S HOUSE

"Go to the potter's house!" There comes a call,
  And, like the prophet, I must needs obey.
  Upon the wheel a shapeless mass of clay
Assumes at once a form symmetrical
Beneath the master's fingers. Slim and tall,
  A lovely vase arises to display

  Its maker's skill, as well it seems it may;
Till, with a suddenness, which must appall,
The potter crushes it in one sharp blow.
  A hidden flaw has caused its swift return
To former state. Fresh turns the wheel, and lo!
  A perfect bowl is formed. Thus I discern
The hand of God, Who only will destroy
To make anew for His transcendent joy.

GOD'S GREAT DISPLAYS

FOR THE PURPOSE of illustration, let us imagine that we are in a large exhibition hall, and that on each of the four sides there is a display stand. Then let us imagine a further display stand in the entrance hall. One has to pass this stand in order to get into the main exhibition itself.

The four displays in the main hall are God's own displays, but first let us look closer at this stand in the entrance. On it there is just one figure, one exhibit. It is the apostle Paul, and this display stand is set up by the Lord Jesus. Paul himself describes it in 1 Timothy 1:12-16, where we read,

"Grateful am I to Him Who invigorates me, Christ Jesus, our Lord, for He deems me faithful, assigning me a service, I, who formerly was a calumniator and a persecutor and an outrager: but I was shown mercy, seeing that I do it being ignorant, in unbelief. Yet the grace of our Lord overwhelms, with faith and love in Christ Jesus. Faithful is the saying, and worthy of all welcome, that Christ Jesus came into the world to save sinners, foremost of whom am *I*. But therefore was I shown mercy, that *in me, the foremost, Jesus Christ should be displaying all His patience, for a pattern of those who are about to be believing on Him for life eonian.*"

Did Jesus display His patience with Peter and the other disciples who walked with Him on earth? We have no doubt that Jesus exercised His patience with each and all of them many times, but when it comes to a question of such a display of His patience that it shall be a pattern for His dealings with all others who would afterwards believe in Him for life eonian, then there is only one figure that will fill the stand. Saul of Tarsus had been a murderer—he had persecuted the ecclesia of God and ravaged it; he had persecuted its members to death, binding and giving over both men and women to jail, as he told King Agrippa, "Many of the saints *I* lock up in jails, obtaining authority from the chief priests. Besides, I deposit a ballot to dispatch them"—that is, he voted to have them put to death—"And at all the synagogues, often punishing them, I compelled them to blaspheme. Besides, being exceedingly maddened against them, I persecuted them as far as the outside cities also" (Acts 26:10, 11).

It is the way in which Christ Jesus deals with this one that forms such a grand display of His patience and makes Paul the pattern for all subsequent believers. How can such a desperate character, such a convinced opposer, be converted? Yet he was, and not merely converted, but completely transformed. If the patience of Jesus was such that it could change Saul the outrager and rabid fanatic, into Paul the apostle of grace and peace, then it can transform the most implacable of God's enemies into the greatest friend. In such cases, the grace of our Lord overwhelms, and no one can be said to be beyond the pale or outside the scope of its influence.

This stand at the entrance is Jesus' own display, but now let us enter the main hall and look at God's displays. Shall we be surprised that it is the apostle Paul, who tells us about them? There are four of them. Let the apostle take us round and describe the displays to us. We imagine one stand on each side of the room.

On the first side is a stand crowded with many vessels, like the vessels of a potter, but they are all marred vessels, adapted for destruction. Our guide tells us about them in Romans 9:22, "Now if God, wanting to display His indignation and to make His powerful doings known, carries on with much patience, the vessels of indignation, adapted for destruction..."

God wanting to display His indignation! But we thought that God was love! Why should He want to display His indignation? Because it is an indignation which is vented against *all unrighteousness,* and it is necessary that this indignation shall be displayed in order that all creation may see the terrible consequences of such unrighteousness—may see in fact what sin and rebellion against God can lead to. God does not *delight* in displaying His indignation—He has no delight in the destruction of evildoers or in the death of the wicked—but He realizes that, without such a display as a contrast, He cannot (as the apostle continues) "make known the riches of His glory on the vessels of mercy, which He makes ready before for glory—us, whom He calls also."

Next to this stand, on the second side of the hall, we can imagine another stand, this time containing only a single vessel, but one specially exalted in order that God might *display His power* in it. We read about this vessel in Romans 9:17, "For the scripture is saying to Pharaoh that 'For this selfsame thing I rouse you up, so that I should be displaying in you My power, and so that My name should be published in the entire earth.'"

Was God's power displayed in Pharaoh? To be sure it was, and it was the power exercised against an unrelenting opponent, the power that brought a stubborn enemy to destruction, the power that defeated and annihilated every alien god that Pharaoh worshipped. For Pharaoh at that time was the earthly representative of all false worship, the supporter of every type of alien god, the willing tool of Satan in his antagonism to the one true God. It was not only in the deliverance of Israel that God's power was shown but more particularly in the utter havoc that was wrought upon Pharaoh and everything that Pharaoh represented. It was in Pharaoh that God's power was displayed. It was in the succession of plagues that God brought upon him that God's omnipotence was manifested, directed as they were against the impotent gods that he worshipped. And similar plagues will come again when God lets loose His indignation at the end of this present eon.

So far the exhibit is rather daunting. A hint of mercy, it is true, but we have not seen mercy put on display. But now let us look at the third stand. Here we have again a single exhibit, but this time one of supreme glory, for this is a stand which displays God's righteousness. Our guide tells us of this in Romans 3:21-26,

"Yet now, apart from law, a righteousness of God is manifested (being attested by the law and the prophets), yet a righteousness of God through Jesus Christ's faith, for all, and on all who are believing, for there is no distinction, for all sinned and are wanting of the glory of God.

"Being justified gratuitously in His grace, through the deliverance which is in Christ Jesus (Whom God purposed for a Propitiatory shelter, through faith in His blood, for a *display of His righteousness* because of the passing over of the penalties of sins which occurred before in the forbearance of God), toward the *display of His righteousness* in the current era, for Him to be just and the Justifier of the one who is of the faith of Jesus."

The theme of this stand is God's righteousness, and here, in the death of His Son, it is put on display in a way that it was never displayed before. If we refer back to the first chapter of Romans, where Paul introduces his evangel for the first time, we read, "For a righteousness which is of God is being revealed in it" (1:17). Now, the word translated 'revealed' is the Greek *apokaluptō*, from which we get our English word 'apocalypse,' or 'revelation.' It has the thought of 'taking a cover from,' as you take the cover from a statue when you unveil it. In the Concordant Literal New Testament, whenever this word is used of a person, it is rendered 'unveil' or 'unveiling,' like the Unveiling of Jesus Christ; but when it is used of a thing it is translated 'reveal' or 'revelation.' But what is revelation other than taking the cover away? All truth is concealed in God, Who knows the end from the beginning, until such time as He chooses to uncover it. And here, in the evangel committed to Paul, the righteousness of God is being revealed, unveiled, uncovered, so that it is now seen in all its majesty and glory. Let us see what the immediate effect is.

If we look at the scriptures outside of the writings of Paul, we find quite a number of people being described as just or righteous. We are thinking of Abel, Lot, John the Baptist, Zechariah and Elizabeth, Joseph, Simeon, Joseph of Arimathea, to name a few. But when once the evangel committed to Paul is proclaimed, what do we find? "Not one is just, not even one." All are brought down to the same common denominator. "All sinned and are wanting of the glory of God" (Rom. 3:10, 23).

Why is this? Because in other parts of Scripture, those who are declared to be just are being compared with the rest of humanity. Abel is just when contrasted with Cain; Lot when constrasted with the people of Sodom; Zechariah when contrasted with the priesthood of his day, as exemplified by, for example, Caiaphas. But when once the righteousness of God (apart from law) is unveiled and put on display, a different standard of comparison is immediately set up, and against this standard all else falls short. All, including Abel and the rest, are reduced to the same level. Not one is just, not even one.

Now we have no doubt that God's righteousness was operating in all His dealings with His creatures.

There can never be unrighteousness with God, and all down the Scriptures men have testified to the righteousness of God. But when it comes to an absolute and open display of God's righteousness that shall stand for all time and be a witness to every creature in earth and heaven, then there is only one exhibit that can fill the stand. In the complete faith-obedience of Jesus Christ, the One truly without sin, the One in Whom no fault could be found at all—in the complete faith-obedience of this One, which brought Him, as the Son of God's love, to the ignominy of the cross and thereby provided a way of deliverance which would enable God, while always remaining just Himself, to justify those of the faith of Jesus—in this is seen an absolute display of God's righteousness which is without parallel elsewhere. And it has an immediate effect—in the current era; for such is the display of God's righteousness through Jesus Christ's faith that God, Who had, in previous times, declared that He would *not* justify the wicked (Ex. 23: 7), can now be seen to be still just while justifying the irreverent, provided that they have the faith of Jesus. In other words, God can take vessels from those adapted for destruction, and by giving them a faith like that of Jesus, declare them righteous in His sight. And that is exactly what He does.

For on this fourth stand, there are quite a lot of vessels, though not nearly so many as there were on the first. They are similar in appearance and in composition to those on the first stand, the vessels of indignation. In themselves, there is nothing to keep them off the first stand. They are of the same clay; they have sinned like the rest, and are wanting of the glory of God; but let us see what Paul says about them in Ephesians 2. This is how he describes them:

"And you, being dead to your offenses and sins, in which once you walked, in accord with the eon of this world, in accord with the chief of the jurisdiction of the air, the spirit now operating in the sons of stubbornness (among whom *we* also all behaved ourselves once in the lusts of our flesh, doing the will of the flesh and of the comprehension, and were, in our nature, children of indignation, even as the rest)''—like all those on that first stand—"yet God, being rich in mercy"—here is where mercy comes to the fore—"because of His vast love with which He loves us (we also being dead to the offenses and the lusts), vivifies us together in Christ (in grace are you saved!) and rouses us together and seats us together among the celestials, in Christ Jesus, that, in the oncoming eons, He *should be displaying the transcendent riches of His grace* in His kindness to us in Christ Jesus. For in grace, through faith, are you saved, and this is not out of you; it is God's approach present, not of works, lest anyone should be boasting. For His achievement are we, being created in Christ Jesus for good works, which God makes ready beforehand, that we should be walking in them."

Here, then, we have it. Here we are among the celestials, where all the troubles of the universe originated. Here we are being used by God to display to them the riches of His grace. In earlier parts of this study, we suggested that the original rebellion against God occurred among the celestials, long before man was created; and that humanity was an entirely separate creation, made in the image and likeness of Himself, to be the *form* in which God's own Son could come to give up His life for the universe, and remedy what had gone wrong in that higher sphere. Thus humanity is made the vehicle through which the reconciling of the universe is to be effected, even though all efforts of humanity itself are in vain and come to nothing, and it is left to God to provide, in the person of His Son, the one effectual means by which this reconciliation is to be accomplished. For God's Son came in the likeness of humanity, and it was as a Human that He died on the cross, and it is the blood of Christ's cross that brings the peace which is the basis of the reconciliation to God of all that is in heaven and on earth (Col. 1:20).

Christ suffered and died as a Man, and the ecclesia which is His body is also made to pass through the form of humanity, and partake of its weaknesses and failures, its tribulations and afflictions, its sufferings and dying, that it may receive in fullest measure the grace of God. Of itself, the ecclesia can do nothing; its members share the vanity of humanity; they are all sinners and, like Saul of Tarsus, onetime enemies of God. It is God Who calls them and justifies them; it is Christ Who hallows them, that "He should be presenting to Himself a glorious ecclesia, not having spot or wrinkle or any such things, but that it may be holy and flawless" (Eph. 5:27). And it is this ecclesia, holy and flawless in God's sight, which will be used by Him to display the transcendent riches of His grace to the whole of the celestial universe.

And how does God do this? Simply like this: He shows first that we really ought to be on that initial stand—children of indignation, even as the rest; if we had our deserts, that is where we would be, recipients of God's indignation even as was displayed in Pharaoh. But because of the deliverance which is in Christ Jesus, the One in Whom His righteousness is so wonderfully displayed, He is able to take us off that first stand—to rescue us out of the coming indignation—and place us here, on this fourth stand, where He can display His grace. He has been exceptionally kind to us in *not* dealing with us according to our acts; He will be equally kind to others whenever they are willing to accept His kindness. Even now we are proclaiming among our fellows a message of conciliation; we shall continue proclaiming this throughout the oncoming eons until all in heaven and earth are completely reconciled to God. We, members of humanity who have the faith of Jesus, are chosen by God to display to the estranged celestial host the magnitude and the marvel of God's grace; and we do this, not by any works of our own (for God will not have us boasting of our own achievements), but simply by proclaiming to them how God, in removing the barrier of sin through the death of His Son, and thereby destroying all enmity between Himself and us, has been able to create us anew in Christ Jesus.

As God has been gracious to us, so He will be gracious to them. This is the true expectation of the ecclesia, to be used of Him to display His grace to others, that they, in turn, may be truly reconciled to God.

> This is, in truth, our glorious expectation—
> That He will take us, and through us proclaim
> The blessed joys of reconciliation
> Till every creature lauds His glorious Name.

And this is, indeed, the true expectation of creation, for as Paul tells us in Romans 8:19, "For the premonition of the creation is awaiting the unveiling [the revealing, the uncovering] of the sons of God. For to vanity was the creation subjected, not voluntarily, but because of Him Who subjects it, in expectation that the creation itself, also, shall be freed from the slavery of corruption into the glorious freedom of the children of God."

That freedom which we, as sons of God, now enjoy in spirit will ultimately be enjoyed by the whole creation when it is reconciled to God, and this includes the whole of humanity, for God wills all mankind to be saved and to come into a realization of the truth (1 Tim. 2:4). When His purpose is accomplished, there will be no vessels of indignation left on that first stand, nor vessels like Pharaoh on the second. God will dwell with humanity, and they will be His peoples, and He will be their God, and will brush away all tears from their eyes (Rev. 21:3, 4).

But for us, who are chosen to display His grace, a

glory beyond measure in being made like Him Who is our Head lies in the immediate future. No wonder Paul prays in Ephesians 1:18 that we might be able "to perceive what is the expectation of His calling, and what the riches of the glory of the enjoyment of His allotment among the saints." God has a marvelous allotment among the saints; He has placed among us that stupendously transcendent display of His grace which will have the effect of bringing back the whole universe into His fatherly care and love, and in awakening in each of His creatures a love responsive that will delight His heart for evermore. This is the allotment which He has in the saints, the true ecclesia of God, the church which is the body of Christ; and we should be eagerly anticipating and pursuing our place in that allotment, which we shall take up fully when our Lord calls us to meet Him in the air, as Paul tells us in 1 Thessalonians 4: 13-18.

Let us not be among those drowsing when He comes, but be continually living in eager anticipation of that day!

> We are looking, we are list'ning
>   For the coming of the Lord,
> With His loudly sounding trumpet
>   And His own commanding word,
> When He calls His saints together,
>   Bidding sleeping ones arise,
> Ready for that glorious meeting
>   With their Saviour in the skies.
>
> We may not be always certain
>   Whom the Lord has made His own,
> But to Him, Who comes to call them,
>   Each is intimately known,
> And in this we may be happy,
>   When He greets them in the air
> Every member of His body
>   Will assuredly be there.

of our Lord Jesus Christ

We are living, we are longing
  For that moment of delight,
When our earnest expectation
  Will be realized in sight;
When these bodies, frail and failing,
  Will assume celestial powers—
What a prospect, what a calling,
  What a privilege is ours!

Designated in God's purpose
  For a grand and glorious place,
To display in future ages
  All the riches of His grace
In His loving kindness to us,
  Which to all will be made known—
How in grace alone He saves us
  Through no merit of our own.

We are watching, we are waiting
  For that long expected sound
That will call us to His presence,
  And to joys that will abound,
In an instant, in a moment,
  In the twinkle of an eye,
Changed from weakness into glory
  For that gathering on high.

This the summit of our blessings,
  To be ever with the Lord,
And to wear the glorious likeness
  Of the One we have adored;
Then throughout His Father's kingdom
  For God's glory we shall shine,
With a splendor all transcendent
  And a radiance Divine.

THE ALL-SUFFICIENCY OF GOD

IN PREVIOUS STUDIES we have consistently stressed the vanity of human endeavor; and in contrast to this must stand the all-sufficiency of God, which we would now like to examine in more detail. What do we understand by the "all-sufficiency of God"?

It is a theme seldom given the importance it deserves. We suppose that, if pressed, we would all admit that God is all-sufficient in Himself and needs no help whatever from any source outside of Himself. But how many of us have turned such an admission into a strong conviction that will govern our actions and our lives? Yet this is what God would have us all do, and what He is gradually training us all to believe. And as this belief grows, so too does the parallel conviction, namely that we, as distinct from God, are neither self-sufficient nor all-sufficient. Rather we do need a source outside of ourselves to be constantly sustaining us.

God is all-sufficient in Himself to accomplish everything that He desires. If He invites our co-operation or engages our services in the furtherance of His designs, it is by favor only, and not because we have something to offer that otherwise He would have to do without. He first puts into us what He requires from us. Thus we are tools or instruments in His hands, fashioned by Him for the use for which He requires us.

There comes a time in our lives when we are called upon to make an *adjustment to our beliefs*. This adjustment can be concisely stated in a few lines of verse, which are quoted simply because they make absolutely clear the meaning of the message we desire to pass on to you.

> Once I esteemed myself, and proudly thought
>   I could help God, His purpose to fulfill—
>   That He had need of me to speak His will,
> Or He might lose the very ones He sought.
> But through my many failures I was taught
>   That He is all-sufficient to instill
>   His thoughts in men without my puny skill—
> That He, in fact, is all, and I am naught.
> And in this revelation I rejoice;
>   A fresh perspective in my life unfolds,
>   As in my thinking God takes rightful place.
> Not merely His the method and the choice,
>   But all the doing, too, as each He molds
>   Into a vessel to display His grace.

Not merely His the method and the choice, but all the doing, too! He is not only the Architect, the Designer, but the Builder also—the Craftsman, the Potter, molding each of His creatures into a vessel to display, not its own glory, but the glory and the grace of the One Who is molding it.

This, then, is our theme—the all-sufficiency of God, and we begin by asking, "Where is the first mention of this in the Scriptures?" Where in His Word does God first reveal Himself to humanity as the All-sufficient One?

Before we try to answer this question, let us make it a little easier. In the King James (Authorized) Version, the Hebrew word that means "All-sufficient" is invariably translated "Almighty," and every time we find the word "Almighty" in the Old Testament, it is the Hebrew *Shaddai*, meaning *All-sufficient*. "I am the Almighty God," means, "I am the God Who suffices."

Our question, therefore, comes down to this: "Where, in the Old Testament, do we find the first use of the word *Almighty*?" When we find that, we shall discover that a completely new truth is being brought to our notice.

Altogether, the word is used 48 times, but these are not spread at all evenly through the Hebrew Scriptures. In only two books does the word occur more than twice, namely Genesis where it occurs six times, and Job where significantly it occurs no less than thirty-one times. Yes, it is to Job, in all his afflictions and sufferings, that God is most often presented as the One Who is all-sufficient. Does not this teach us that afflictions and sufferings are pressed upon us in order that God, in all His sufficiency, may be fully appreciated? And that we, in all our distresses, may fully turn to Him, and like Paul may come to learn that His grace is sufficient for us? Are not all the experiences of this life granted to us in order that we may grow into a deeper appreciation of God? That like Job we may come to say, "I have heard of Thee by the hearing of the ear: but now mine eye seeth Thee"? This was the culmination of Job's experience, and the result was that he came to abhor himself and repented in dust and ashes, whereupon God blessed him by giving him twice as much as he had before.

But now let us go right back to the first occurrence of the word Almighty (*Shaddai*). It occurs in Genesis 17:1, where God appears to Abram and says, "I am the Almighty God. Walk thou before Me, and be thou perfect." ("I am the Al-Who-Suffices. Walk before Me and become flawless"—CV).

This is a remarkable statement, especially when we realize that humanity had been on this earth well over 3,000 years before God took one of their number aside and introduced Himself *for the first time* as "the One Who Suffices." (This figure of over 3,000 years is based on the ages of the patriarchs as given in the Septuagint

Version of Genesis 5 and Genesis 11, and as carried forward into the CV).

Let us then look at some of the circumstances around the life of Abram and see why God chose this particular moment to introduce Himself to humanity in this way.

Abram, or Abraham, is one of the really great characters of the Scriptures; yet not great because of anything that he himself was able to do to achieve greatness, but great because God made him so.

He it was to whom God said, "And I will make you into a great nation, and I will bless you and make your name great, and you must become a blessing" (Gen. 12:2, CV). Again, he it was of whom the Scriptures declare that he believed God, and God reckoned it to him for righteousness (*cf* Gen. 15:6).

So important is this last truth that it is carried over into three separate places in the Greek Scriptures, being brought to our notice twice by Paul and once by James. Paul introduces it into both his Roman and Galatian epistles, and in each of these two cases it is made clear that it was not written just for Abraham alone, but that also, in some strange way, it has an application to others (including ourselves) if they have the same kind of faith that Abraham had.

The relevant passages are Romans 4:16-25 and Galatians 3:5-9. In Romans it is stated that "it was not written because of him [Abraham] only, but because of us also," while in Galatians it is affirmed that "those of faith are being blessed together with believing Abraham."

To see what these statements mean, we must examine some of Abraham's experiences, particularly those relating to his faith in God. We shall then learn why God reveals Himself to him as the One-Who-Suffices, and thus see how this applies to us also. So let us not hesitate to delve into the Hebrew Scriptures and see what they have to tell us about Abraham.

We find him very early in the scriptural narrative, between the eleventh and twenty-fifth chapters of the first book, Genesis. We first meet him at the age of 75, and he dies at the age of 175. Thus, that part of his life which is portrayed in Scripture is exactly 100 years, and of that 100 years, the first 25 are undoubtedly the most momentous, as laying the foundation of all that followed.

When we are first introduced to him, he is called *Abram* and is living in the ancient city of Ur in Chaldea or Mesopotamia. About that time, Ur was the most magnificent city in all the world, a center of manufacture, farming and shipping in a land of immense fertility and wealth. But it was also a heathen city with many gods and goddesses. The principal deity of Ur was Sin, the moon-god, whose wife Ningal or Nina, was the one after whom the city of Nineveh was named.

Thus we have the background of Abraham's early life and upbringing, a city of wealth and prosperity allied to that which always goes with worldly fortune, namely false worship. That Abraham himself was affected by it can scarcely be in doubt, for Joshua tells us that "even Terah, the father of Abraham...*served other gods*" (Josh. 24:2). Even after Abraham had been called away from Ur, his relatives in the east continued to worship idols, for in the time of his great-nephew Laban, we find Rachel, Laban's daughter, causing trouble by stealing and hiding her father's gods (Gen. 31:30-35).

It may come as a shock to realize that the direct line of descent from Adam, which had been kept flawless up to the time of Noah (Gen. 6:9), had now become contaminated by idolatry. Was there any righteous, God-fearing man in the world at this time? Might it not then have been true, as the Psalmist wrote many years afterwards, "The fool hath said in his heart, There is no God. They are corrupt, they have done abominable works, there is none that doeth good. The Lord looked down

from heaven upon the children of men, to see if there
were any that did understand, and seek God. They are
all gone aside, they are altogether become filthy; there
is none that doeth good, no, not one" (Ps. 14:1-3).
This passage was later quoted by Paul in his Roman
epistle as his summing up of the general sinfulness of
mankind and the consequent vanity and ineffectiveness
of human endeavor. Might it not have been particularly
true in Abram's time?

It had earlier been said of Noah that he was a just
man, flawless in his generations and that he walked with
God. Alone of all humanity, *he was the only one of
whom this could be said at that time;* it was true of none
else, for all but he and his family were destroyed because
of their wickedness. But what had been said of Noah
could not be said of Terah, Abram's father; and if it
could not be said of him, where was there a man who
was not touched by idolatry?

The plain fact is that humanity, when not indwelt by
the vivifying Spirit of God, soon becomes exceedingly
sinful because of the domination of the flesh. "The
disposition of the flesh is enmity to God," says Paul,
"for it is not subject to the law of God, for neither is it
able. Now those who are in the flesh are not able to
please God" (Rom. 8:7,8). He is aware that good is
not making its home in him, that is, in his flesh (Rom.
7:18). Jeremiah tells us that "the heart is deceitful
above all things, and desperately wicked" (Jer. 17:9).

The tendency of humanity is naturally toward wickedness, for death reigns over all. After the race had been
in existence for more than 2,000 years (according to the
Septuagint Version), and had had plenty of opportunity
to prove itself, God saw that the wickedness of men was
so great and the thoughts of their hearts so evil that He
decided to bring the eon to an end with a deluge that
would destroy all except the one family of Noah. Noah
and his sons were preserved to continue the race, not

because the race deserved a second chance, but because God's purpose still needed humanity as the vehicle in which His Son should come to give His life for the universe. No, far from humanity deserving a second chance, the deluge was God's judgment upon it. Here He plainly showed that all the efforts of men led only to vanity and destruction; indeed, so wicked was humanity that the preaching of Noah could make no converts. In the midst of a world of iniquity Noah was a heralder of righteousness.

HUMANITY'S INSUFFICIENCY

Therefore, as we have stated above, mankind failed, yet God gave humanity a fresh start with Noah, repeating to him the commands that He had originally given to Adam (*cf* Gen. 1:28 and Gen. 9:1). But it soon became apparent that iniquity was abounding again, and at the tower of Babel God scattered mankind and confused their languages (disintegrating their lip) to put a restraint upon them. Still things grew worse, and by the time we come to Terah and Abram, humanity was just about as bad again as it was in the days of Noah. This is shown by the fact that, when God determined to destroy Sodom and Gomorrah because of their wickedness, only Lot and his two daughters were saved, despite the promise to Abraham that the city would be spared if as few as ten righteous people could be found within it. But, like Noah, Lot had made no converts.

Over and over again, we find humanity turning to idolatry and wickedness whenever God withdraws His restraining influence. Even Israel, the descendants of Abraham, revert many times to the idolatry of their ancestors, and God has to keep chiding them. The Gentile nations are no better. In all this, we find history continually repeating itself. The iniquity of the Amalekites; the wickedness of Nineveh; the unbelief and perversity of the generation living at the time of the Lord's

first coming; the wickedness and violence of the end
time of this eon which we are now seeing and which is
likened to the days of Noah; and the rebellion which will
break out again among humanity at the end of the
millennium when the Adversary is loosed for a little
season and the restraints of the righteous reign of Christ
are withdrawn—all these are evidences of the inherent
unrighteousness of humanity which makes it *impossible*
for anything in the flesh to please God. Even the
righteous reign of Christ does not change the inherent
evil tendencies of humanity; it only supresses them.
Only a *new creation* can change them.

And so we are suggesting that when Abram was called,
there was none righteous, no, not one—not even Abram.
He was like the rest, but God appeared to him in Ur of
the Chaldees and commanded him to leave his home and
go forth into a land that God would show him. And
Abram, an idolater, obeyed the voice of the one true
God. Such is the superiority of the power of God over
that of the idols that Abram and his companions wor-
shiped. Henceforth *Abram* would only worship the God
that condescended and elected to be called the God of
Abraham.

In Genesis 12 we find Abram at the age of 75 moving
into the land of Canaan, accompanied by Sarai, his wife,
and his nephew Lot. But things were not immediately
made easy for him. Firstly there was the opposition of
the native inhabitants, for we read that the Canaanite
was still dwelling in the land (Gen. 12:6). Then
secondly there was a famine in the land (v. 10), and this
was so grievous as to cause Abram to seek succor in
Egypt. Evidently he did not realize that when God
gave him the land He gave him all that was in it and
that included the famine. Abram should have stayed
where he was and trusted in God to provide. But God
had not yet revealed Himself to Abram as the All-
sufficient One, and Abram relied on his own judgment.

This is the first mention of Egypt in the Scriptures, and what an eventful incident this proved to be. Quite apart from the fact that Abram, through trusting in himself, got into difficulties and needed the intervention of God to extricate him, it was probably during this sojourn in Egypt that Sarai obtained the services of Hagar, her Egyptian maid, who was to become the mother of Ishmael, and indeed the mother of all the Arabs. And the consequences of this are still to be observed today in the animosity of the Arab states to Israel.

Then thirdly there was the trouble within his own family—the dissention with Lot which led to continuous strife between their respective herdsmen, so that Abram deemed it desirous that they should separate. This was followed by a kind of tribal war in the land during which Lot was captured, and Abram and his servants went in force to deliver him.

And fourthly there was the doubt within himself as to whether God was able to fulfill His promise or not. Or did He require some action on Abram's part, on the basis of the popular idea today, "God helps those who help themselves"? Abram had been assured by God that though at the moment he had no child, his heir would not be a mere servant, high and respected though that servant might be, but that one who was born of himself would be his heir. But then the question arose, Was Sarai too old? They both assumed so, and after they had lived in Canaan ten years Sarai decided that something must be done about it, and she gave Abram her Egyptian maid Hagar to wife. As a result of this mistaken endeavor to assist God, Ishmael was born, and there is no doubt that for the next thirteen years Ishmael was growing up as Abram's son, and in Abram's mind as the heir of the promise. Remember how later on Abraham said to God, "O that Ishmael should live before Thee!" (Gen. 17:18).

The last verse of Genesis 16 tells us that Abram was
86 years old when Ishmael was born, and the first verse
of the next chapter tells us that he was 99 years old
when the Lord next appeared to him and introduced
Himself as the God Who is All-sufficient: "I am the
Al-Who-Suffices. Walk before Me and become flawless."

What is the meaning of this? What is the reason for
it? The next few verses give the answer. God is now
taking over and is going to show Abram that He is all-
sufficient in Himself to keep His promises however dif-
ficult or even impossible they may seem to human eyes.
Seven times in the next few verses God tells Abram
what He is doing or going to do, and all that is required
of Abram is that he should believe—nothing else. The
All-sufficient God will make him fruitful beyond measure, and in conformity with this his name is henceforth
to be Abraham, for says God, "the forefather of a throng
of nations *I* have made you." *Abram* means "exalted
father"; *Abraham,* "exalted father of a throng."

But God did then ask Abraham to do something rather
peculiar; He asked him to circumcise himself and also
stipulated that all the male children of his seed should
be circumcised too. And this was to be the sign of
the covenant that God was making with him. And how
is this covenant a sign? How could this peculiar rite
be a confirmation of a covenant?

Only in one way; this is by signifying that the flesh
could achieve nothing. The casting away of a portion
of flesh was symbolic of the worthlessness of the whole
flesh to achieve anything that God desired. The flesh
could only produce an Ishmael, a son inevitably subject
to the bondage of the flesh—Ishmael was the son of a
bondwoman; but God could achieve an Isaac, a son that
was not subject to bondage at all, a son of a freewoman.
All this is allegorical, as Paul told the Galatians. It is
true that in everything that effects humanity the flesh
can only produce that which is subject to the bondage

of sin, for sin is now an inbred part of flesh; but God operating through the flesh can produce that which is free from all such bondage and therefore pleasing to Himself. This principle is as true today as it was in Abraham's time.

And Abraham at last came to recognize this as we see when the narrative continues. In Genesis 17:15 we find God changing Sarai's name to Sarah and promising Abraham a son of her. Abraham's immediate reaction was to fall on his face and laugh and say in his heart, "To one a hundred years of age shall a son be born? And should Sarah, ninety years of age, be bearing?" He was still a bit unsure and said to God, "O that Ishmael should live before Thee!" But God reiterated His previous statement and said, "Nevertheless, behold, Sarah, your wife is bearing you a son, and you shall call his name Isaac. And I set up My covenant with him for a covenant eonian, and with his seed after him." And then after a comforting word for Abraham concerning Ishmael, God for the third time emphasizes the covenant which He would establish with Isaac by repeating that Sarah would bear him the following year.

We notice the change of name from Sarai to Sarah by means of the Hebrew letter corresponding to our letter 'h.' It is the same letter that was inserted in Abram's name to change it to Abraham; the fifth letter of the Hebrew alphabet in each case (five is the number of grace). From simply being one held in high regard, she is to become a Chiefess, a mother of nations. Twice more in the next chapter the Lord was to repeat the promise concerning Sarah, making five times in all— three times to Abraham alone and twice to Abraham within Sarah's hearing. Abraham had laughed and Sarah had laughed, both in incredulity, but God challenged them both with a searching question, "Is anything too hard for the Lord?" (AV). "Is anything too marvelous for Ieue Alueim?" (CV).

God was to change their laughter of incredulity into a
laughter of joy by giving them a son whose name was to
be "Laugh-causer," for that is the literal meaning of
Isaac. But for this to happen, Abraham had to accept
God as the All-sufficient One, the One Who could accomplish all without any help from outside. And this is
exactly what Paul brings to our notice in Romans 4
when he speaks of this episode in Abraham's life. Beginning at verse 16 we read:

"Therefore it is of faith that it may accord with grace,
for the promise to be confirmed to the entire seed, not to
those of the law only, but to those also of the faith of
Abraham, who is father of us all, according as it is
written that, A father of many nations have I appointed
you—facing which, he believes it of the God Who is
vivifying the dead and calling what is not as if it were—
who, being beyond expectation, believes in expectation,
for him to become the father of many nations, according
to that which has been declared, 'Thus shall be your
seed.' And, not being infirm in faith, he considers his
own body, already deadened (being inherently somewhere about a hundred years) and the deadening of the
matrix of Sarah, yet the promise of God was not doubted
in unbelief, but he was invigorated by faith, giving glory
to God, being fully assured also, that, what He has
promised, He is able to do also. Wherefore, also, it is
reckoned to him for righteousness."

God had said to Abram, "I am the God Who suffices.
Walk before Me and become flawless." Abram, his
name now changed to Abraham, believed and trusted
God implicitly and in so doing became *the father of all
who believe.*

What a wonderful title this is! The father of all who
believe. In a world completely full of idolatry, Abraham
stands out as the one who believed. But surely the title
conveys more than this. Abel believed God, Enoch believed God, Noah believed God. All these come before

Abraham in the list of characters of faith in Hebrews 11. Then why is not one of these the *father* of all who believe? The answer lies in the fact that to none of these did God introduce Himself as the All-sufficient God. To Noah for example God did not introduce Himself in that way; if He had, He would have provided the ark for Noah. Instead, Noah was encouraged to believe that he had to do quite a lot himself to ensure his salvation—he had to build the ark which took considerable time and labor. But to Abraham God introduced Himself as the God Who suffices—the God Who is prepared to do all, even to the extent of vivifying the dead and calling what is not as though it were; and it is because Abraham believed· such a God that he is "the father of all who believe."

In other words, *a new conception has been introduced into believing.* No longer is it a case of "God helps those who help themselves," but "God helps those who *cannot* help themselves." And there are none that can help themselves, for the sum total of all human endeavor is just "vanity." And such a believing provides the basis for a reckoning of righteousness.

But it was not written because of Abraham alone that righteousness is reckoned to him, "but because of us also, to whom it is about to be reckoned, who are believing on Him Who rouses Jesus our Lord from among the dead, Who was given up because of our offenses, and was roused because of our justifying. Being, then, justified by faith, we may be having peace toward God, through our Lord, Jesus Christ."

The evangel of the all-sufficiency of God was preached before to Abraham so that he should recognize that the outworking of God's promises depended upon Him alone, and God reveals Himself to us in exactly the same way through his apostle Paul. Does not Paul say in 2 Cor. 5:14:

"For the love of Christ is constraining us, judging

this, that, if One died for the sake of all, consequently
all died. And He died for the sake of all that those who
are living should by no means still be living to themselves, but to the One dying and being roused for their
sakes. So that we, from now on, *are acquainted with
no one according to flesh*—'' the flesh is being cast aside,
even as God, in the figure of circumcision, demonstrated
to Abraham—''Yet, even if we have known Christ according to flesh, nevertheless now we know Him so no
longer'' Why? Because Christ has given up His flesh
at Golgotha. ''So that, if anyone is in Christ, there is
a new creation''—and we ask at this point, Who is the
creator of the new creation? Surely, it is God: He is
the Creator of the new just as He was the Creator of the
old. Did humanity have any say in its own creation?
Do we have any say in the creating of ourselves anew?
''If anyone is in Christ, there is a new creation: the
primitive passed by. Lo! there has come new! YET ALL
IS OF GOD, Who conciliates us to Himself through Christ.''

''YET ALL IS OF GOD,'' says Paul. ''I AM THE GOD
WHO SUFFICES,'' God said to Abraham. Can we accept
the spiritual fact that in our salvation and in our lives
all is of God, and not try to adulterate the completeness
of His work in us by trying to intrude a little of our
own efforts?

Augustus Toplady summed up the position when he
wrote:

> Not the labors of my hands,
> Can fulfil the law's demands;
> Could my zeal no respite know,
> Could my tears forever flow,
> All for sin could not atone:
> Thou must save, and Thou alone.
> Nothing in my hand I bring,
> Simply to Thy cross I cling;
> Naked, come to Thee for dress,
> Helpless, look to Thee for grace.

Paul too summed it up when he wrote in Ephesians 2:8-10, "For in grace, through faith, are you saved, and this is *not out of you;* it is God's approach present, not of works, lest anyone should be boasting. For *His* achievement are we, being created in Christ Jesus for good works, which God makes ready beforehand, that we should be walking in them."

"Walk before Me and become flawless," God said to Abraham. "We to be holy and flawless in His sight," wrote Paul (Eph. 1:4). Let this ever be our attitude to God that we recognize Him as the One Who Suffices as well as the One Who Supplies, for *all* is of Him.

FROM ABRAM TO ABRAHAM

IN THIS SERIES of studies it has been suggested that the real reason for the creation of humanity was that it might provide a form in which it would be possible for our Lord to come and give His life for the universe.

That is why man was made in the image and likeness of God—that Jesus could come in human guise and still be recognized as the Son of God. Both Peter and Nathaniel testified to this fact (Matt. 16:16; John 1:49). Humanity was created in order to provide the vehicle, namely flesh, in which death could operate. But why the need for this? Because prior to the creation of humanity there had been a rebellion against God among His higher creations—His prime creations—the inhabitants of the celestial realms. How do we know this? How do we know that there had been a rebellion among the celestials?

Because (1) we are told in Ephesians 6 that our adversaries are not blood and flesh but that we wrestle with "the sovereignties, with the authorities, with the world-mights of this darkness, with the *spiritual forces of wickedness among the celestials.*" Because (2) we are told, in Colossians 1:20 that the reconciliation work accomplished by the blood of Christ's cross must include those in heaven as well as those on earth. Because (3) there must be new heavens as well as a new earth, and the creation of new heavens would be unnecessary if the original heavens had remained unsullied. Because (4) we are told that the original creation of the heavens and the earth was followed by a darkness accompanied by chaos and disruption (Gen. 1:2), and this was before man appeared on the scene at all. Because (5) we are told that the Lambkin was slain from the disruption of the world (*kosmos*), and this again was before man was created. Therefore, the slain Lambkin was a factor in God's purpose before humanity appeared, and humanity was, in fact, the means created by which the figurative Lambkin could be slain.

But it soon became clear that humanity in its own powers could achieve nothing. The first generation from Adam provided clear proof of this—Eve's firstborn showed himself to be a murderer, and in this typified all humanity who would rather crucify the Saviour than acclaim Him. We have already traced the failure of humanity up to the deluge when it was all but destroyed —so complete was God's judgment against it—and through to the time of Abram when it was again in an idolatrous state. But we have also seen how with *Abram*, representative of idolatrous mankind, God took His stand before humanity and indeed in front of all creation, and declared, "I am the God Who suffices." And *Abraham* believed God and became the father of all who believe— the first in an entirely new concept of believing. The first to believe that ALL IS OF GOD.

The lesson of mankind teaches us that humanity was completely unable to save itself, let alone provide the Saviour of the universe for which purpose it had been created. This is because of the inherent nature of flesh which is a form of creation especially adapted for the sufferings of death. Yet this very feature which inhibits its own power to perform a useful service for God is the one which God actually uses to fulfil His purpose. For God will not be balked; He cannot be thwarted. He does nothing in vain. He created humanity as an instrument for His use, and full use will be made of that instrument. Though thousands of years might elapse, during which men would seek in vain for a Saviour from among themselves, God Himself would eventually provide the One Who as the seed of the woman would bruise the serpent's head. The God Who suffices would produce in humanity the One Whom Isaac portrayed and thereby turn the grief of the universe into laughter. Humanity, in the person of the virgin Mary, merely confirmed the form in which that Saviour should come.

There are many sincere people claiming to be believers who yet pay homage to the virgin Mary. This is surely misplaced worship. Mary declared herself to be blessed simply because she was privileged to be the mother of the promised Messiah. She was the one chosen by God to bring Him into the world and to provide Him with His body of flesh, but His Father was God. He was generated by the Spirit of God, not by man. The widespread adoration of a woman only presses home the fact of man's incapability. Mary was blessed (happy) in the role that she was called upon to play; but to exalt her to a place of veneration is to deny the all-sufficiency of God Who alone could provide the Lamb that should take away sin.

Yes, it was God Who sent "His own Son in the likeness of sin's flesh" (Rom. 8:3). It is God Who (to use the Greek aorist tense, which takes no account of time) "thus loves the world, so that He gives His only-begotten Son." It is God Who "is commending this love of His to us, seeing that, while we are still sinners, Christ died for our sakes" (Rom. 5:8). But Christ Himself was fully obedient to the will of God. He took "the form of a slave" and came to be "in the likeness of humanity" and was "found in fashion as a man" (Phil. 2:7,8).

Jesus frequently called Himself "the Son of Mankind." He was a Man in the fullest sense of the word. (See 1 Cor. 15:47; 1 Tim. 2:5). He had all the feelings of humanity and could sympathize with its infirmities (Heb. 4:15). He could hunger (Matt. 4:2), be weary

(John 4:6), experience suffering (Matt. 16:21), and weep in compassion for the sufferings of others (John 11:35). He needed to be taught, for in fact He learned obedience through that which He suffered (Heb. 5:8). Like Adam He could be tried by the Adversary, and if He came through the trial without sin it was not because of any superiority of His flesh, but simply because His flesh was completely dominated by His Spirit which He had received from God.

And yet though Jesus lived a life in the flesh which was completely without sin, this does not glorify the flesh but rather glorifies God Who was operating in Him. Frequently Jesus said that He could do nothing of Himself, but only the works of His Father. Even in the hour of His greatest trial He glorified God by the very nature of the death that He would die (John 12:27-33).

With the crucifixion of Christ, the flesh fulfilled the main function for which it had been created. It is the lot of the flesh to be crucified, deadened, discarded. "Those of Christ Jesus crucify the flesh together with its passions and lusts" (Gal. 5:24). The rite of circumcision signified the casting off of the flesh as impotent; the Jews, with the perversity of humanity, misread the sign and regarded it as a symbol of physical superiority. How can mutilation ever be an improvement? Those who glorify the flesh are enemies of the cross of Christ. Paul had no confidence in the flesh, but rather looked upon it and its apparent accomplishments and advantages as something to be discarded and treated as refuse that he might gain Christ and be found in Him (see Phil. 3:1-16).

What, then, should be our attitude toward the flesh? We should regard it as nothing but a temporary earthen vessel to be discarded in that day when Christ shall call us to Himself and make us like Himself, that we may display to all in the celestial realms the transcendent riches of the grace of a God Who suffices.

It is only as we believe in such a God that we grow into a deeper realization of Himself which is what Paul's epistles are consistently urging. When we accept that ALL IS OF GOD and refuse to adulterate His power of salvation by mixing it with human endeavor, we can truly say like Job, "I have heard of Thee by the hearing of the ear, but *now* mine eye seeth Thee." The evangel is *God's* power for salvation based upon the heralding of the cross of Christ, and when truly appreciated produces laughter and rejoicing in our hearts, for nothing can turn it to sorrow.

Going back for a moment to the circumstances surrounding Abraham, it is significant that God chose Ishmael's name as well as Isaac's. Ishmael means "God is hearing"; Isaac means "Producing laughter." God indicated that He had heard the groans of Hagar by naming her expected child Ishmael; but His real answer to her groans lay in a laughter-producing Isaac. That is why He directed her back to her mistress (Gen. 16). Later He was to hear the groans of a sorely afflicted Israel and provide an answer in a delivering Moses so that they would all sing together, "The Lord is my strength and song, and He is become my salvation" (Ex. 15:2). And make no mistake, God has also heard the groans of a sorrowing universe—a universe estranged from Him, an entire creation groaning and travailing together until now—and He has provided His answer in the One Whom both Isaac and Moses typified, a laughter-producing and delivering Christ.

God intends all His creatures to enjoy themselves. He wants them to laugh and sing. He has no pleasure in groans and tears. Indeed He has promised to wipe away every tear and to abolish completely that which causes misery (Rev. 21:4). But first He hears the groans and then proceeds to remove the cause for groaning. He allows the trial and then provides the sequel (1 Cor. 10:13). Yet in one sense He provides the sequel

first, for everything was purposed from the beginning.
Though it is true that the Lambkin was slain *from* the
disruption of the world (Rev. 13:8), it is equally true
that the blood of Christ as of a flawless and unspotted
Lamb was foreknown, indeed, *before* the disruption of
the world (1 Pet. 1:20). God's purpose in every facet
and detail was planned from the outset, and in no sense
whatever is any part of it an improvisation to meet an
emergency. He is the One Who tells "from the beginning the hereafter, and from aforetime, what has not yet
been done, saying, All My counsel shall be confirmed, and
all My desire will I do" (Isa. 46:10). He is "the One
Who is operating all in accord with the counsel of His
will" (Eph. 1:11) and Who has purposed "to head up
all in the Christ—both that in the heavens and that on
the earth," and "through Him, to reconcile all to Him
(making peace through the blood of His cross) whether
those on the earth or those in the heavens" (Eph. 1:10;
Col. 1:20).

When the reconciliation of all is complete the joy of
the universe will be full. When the purpose of the All-
sufficient God has reached its consummation, and He is
All in all, every heart will be filled with the true laughter
which accompanies the praise and adoration of Him Who
is Supreme and Whose name is Love.

.   .   .   .

We have entitled this particular study, "From Abram
to Abraham," because we wish to stress the importance
of this change of name. It represents a turning-point
in God's relations with humanity, and indeed with
creation as a whole; it indicates the moment at which
God determines to make a new and all-important revelation of Himself; it marks the point at which He introduces an additional value into believing.

We may, therefore, properly ask ourselves a significant
question. As believers, do we classify ourselves with

Abram or with *Abraham*? *Abram* means "exalted father," and at first sight may seem to be a name worthy of great respect, but it was the man-given name which he held in idolatry and which he continued to hold right up to the moment when God appeared to him as the One-Who-Suffices. At that moment his name was changed to *Abraham*, meaning "exalted father of a throng," and he became the father of all who believe. Now with which name do we associate ourselves? For by just as much as we introduce self-glory, self-righteousness or self-endeavor into our relationship with God, by so much do we become idolaters, for by so much are we paying homage to the flesh. This is what *Abram* was doing. "But," says Paul, "Those of faith, these are sons of *Abraham*" (Gal. 3:7).

Let us not fall back into the former category, but rather let us give all glory to God, abhorring self completely, regarding the flesh as being dead, and consequently worthless; then, believing God as the All-sufficient One we shall, as those of faith, be blessed together with believing Abraham. We shall be blessed as Abraham was with the righteousness of God, for this is only reckoned to us when we believe. And "being, then, justified [declared righteous] by faith, we may be having peace toward God, through our Lord Jesus Christ, through Whom we have the access also by faith into this grace in which we stand, and we may be glorying in expectation of the glory of God" (Rom. 5:1,2).

We were sinners, and like all the rest of humanity were wanting of the glory of God. He, the One-Who-Suffices, rescues us from this position by the giving up of His own Son, and as we believe on Him Who rouses our Lord Jesus from among the dead, so we are justified. No longer are we then walking according to flesh but according to spirit, and God's Spirit is making its home in us.

Let us, then, like our father in faith, Abraham, walk

before God, acknowledging Him in all things as the One-Who-Suffices, and cast aside the deeds of the flesh as worthless and refuse; thus shall we be holy and flawless in His sight, and thus shall we find in our lives, even while still in the flesh, the joy and peace that come with believing. For no longer being debtors to the flesh, but living in accord with the spirit, we shall indeed know that we are sons of God.

May God bless us to this end, and in addition to the joy and peace, give us all laughter and rejoicing in the knowledge that He is operating in us to will as well as to work for the sake of His delight.

A UNIQUE TREASURE CHEST

HAVE you ever possessed a treasure chest? A real treasure chest? A chest with fabulous wealth inside?

We have such a chest in mind. It is a most remarkable one. It is in two almost equal parts, as though divided down the middle. From the outside it does not seem anything exceptional, but when it is opened its contents are found to be priceless. Each part has a key which is built into it—a kind of combination lock. If you know the key phrase, you can open the compartment. The first one is full of dazzling pictures in gold frames. No human being has ever seen the like of them elsewhere. The second compartment may seem, by comparison, fairly dull, as though it contained parchments rather than pictures. But when examined closely, these are found to be equally priceless, for they tell us how we should act when the pictures come into our possession.

By now you will perhaps have realized that the chest we are talking about is the epistle to the Ephesians, which is divided into two almost equal parts of three chapters each. Although the division into chapters is man-made, the two parts of the epistle are clearly marked, as each ends with the word, "Amen." This indicates that the contents of each part of the letter are genuine—there are no fakes in this chest. The word "Amen" is from the Hebrew; it means "faithful"; at the beginning of a sentence it is translated, "Verily"; when it comes at the end it is left in its Hebrew form, "Amen." Verily indeed, the whole of the contents of this epistle is a faithful declaration of a faithful God.

The first part of the letter deals with teaching, the second part with deportment or behavior. The first three chapters describe our wealth, or riches, in Christ; the second three, our *walk* in the Lord. And what about the keys to open each part? Well, the keys are built into the beginning of each section. The key to the part describing our *wealth* in Christ is the passage in the first chapter beginning, "Blessed be the God and Father of our Lord Jesus Christ, Who blesses us with every spiritual blessing among the celestials in Christ, according as He chooses us in Him before the disruption of the world, we to be holy and flawless in His sight." The key to the part outlining our true walk in the Lord is the passage at the beginning of the fourth chapter, "I am entreating you, then, I, the prisoner in the Lord, to walk worthily of the calling with which you were called."

If we can appreciate the meaning of these two keys, and turn them correctly, we shall have gone a long way toward a clearer understanding of this epistle, and indeed of God's purpose of the eons. For there, buried deeply in the inner recesses of the chest, is a phrase which occurs only once in the whole of God's Word, *the purpose of the eons.* It is a phrase of inestimable value, for it throws further light on the theme of our studies, the place of humanity in God's purpose. Let us read the passage where it occurs, chapter 3, from verse 9.

"...and to enlighten all as to what is the administration of the secret, which has been concealed from the eons in God, Who creates all, that now may be made known to the sovereignties and the authorities among the celestials, through the ecclesia, the multifarious wisdom of God, in accord with the purpose of the eons, which He makes in Christ Jesus, our Lord."

THE PURPOSE OF THE EONS

Only in this one epistle does this gem of a phrase occur. In the epistle to the Romans we find references to the purpose of God, but here in Ephesians it is expanded to include *all the eons.* It stretches from the beginning to the consummation; it embraces everything that is finite. And let us note that this unique phrase of Scripture occurs in a celestial setting. It is *among the celestials* that the wisdom of God is to be made known, and not merely to the lower ones in the celestial realms, but to the very highest of God's creations, the sovereignties and the authorities—those who at present have the rule and power. With the exception of the Lord Himself, there are none more lofty than these. And it is through the ecclesia, which has earlier been defined as the body of Christ, that this revelation of the multifarious wisdom of God is to be made. This is the marvel of it all that through such as us the great ones in God's universe are to learn the lessons He has to teach them. The appreciation of this great truth surely adds new luster to the treasures in our chest.

So now let us see if we can turn the two keys; the one at the beginning of the first chapter which opens the door to our understanding of the greatness of the riches that are ours in Christ, and the one at the beginning of the fourth chapter, which opens the door to a correct appreciation of our walk in the Lord. But first let us see how the chest itself came into our possession.

THE PRISONER OF CHRIST JESUS

Many years ago, a traveler, worn and prematurely aged by hardship and affliction, occupied a room in Rome with a warden soldier continually at his side. He had done no wrong, yet he was under perpetual guard. His life had been one of immense activity and peril. In Asia and Europe, as an apostle of Christ, he had carried His message from city to city, proclaiming it zealously wherever he went. His privations and sufferings had been more than enough to break the spirit of any ordinary man. The brutal marks of thrice inflicted Roman rods would never leave his back; five times he had been unjustly and cruelly flogged by his own countrymen; once he had even been stoned, and had miraculously survived. In weariness, in jails, in blows, in deaths—such had been his experiences in a life more than ordinarily energetic. And now his movements were curtailed and his ministry apparently constricted by four walls and a chain. To so restless a soul, such restraint would normally be doubly irksome. Yet from that place of confinement, and from that body scarred and battered and bearing all the marks of unparalleled tribulation, there burst forth with startling suddenness like an eruption from a dormant volcano, a message, the like of which neither earth nor heaven had ever heard before. And both earth and heaven, did they but know it, had an interest in it and were affected by it.

THE FIRST KEY

"Blessed be the God and Father of our Lord Jesus Christ, Who blesses us with every spiritual blessing among the celestials, in Christ, according as He chooses us in Him before the disruption of the world, we to be holy and flawless in His sight, in love designating us beforehand for the place of a son for Him through Christ Jesus; in accord with the delight of His will, for the laud of the glory of His grace, which graces us in the Beloved."

What a message to come out of a prison, and from one who had been so terribly and persistently ill-treated! And what vistas of splendor do these first few treasures in the chest present!

As we read on through the first chapter of this wonderful letter, we see more and more of the marvelous spiritual eonian riches that, through grace, are ours in God's Son. We have "the deliverance through His blood, the forgiveness of offenses in accord with the riches of His grace, which He lavishes on us"; we are made aware of "the secret of His will...to have an administration of the complement of the eras, to head up all in the Christ"; and we find that we have a special place in this, for we are told that our lot was cast in Him, "that we should be for the laud of His [God's] glory, who are pre-expectant in the Christ." That is, we come into our expectation before others can expect to do so.

We notice that in presenting these grand truths to us, the apostle's first thought is one of praise to the God and Father of our Lord Jesus Christ. In fact, it can be truly said that the whole of the passage from verse 3 to verse 14 of this first chapter is one long impassioned outpouring of praise—the longest sustained outflowing of praise anywhere in Paul's writings, as J. Sidlow Baxter points out in his work, EXPLORE THE BOOK (vol. 6, p. 165). Above everything, the treasures in our chest redound to the glory of God, and God is to be praised for them. At first, in verse 6, it is a praise for the glory of His grace, but later, in verses 12 and 14, this develops into a praise for the glory of God Himself.

A PRAYER FOR PERCEPTION

With so many riches in our possession, do we need anything else? Yes, certainly we do. Riches are valueless unless one *knows* their value. With possession must be coupled perception; and so, while the first part of this opening chapter is a praise to God for spiritual possession—we are in possession, by God's grace, of all spiritual blessings—the prayer is for spiritual perception—"for you to *perceive* what is the expectation of His calling, and what the riches of the glory of the enjoyment of His allotment among the saints, and what the transcendent greatness of His power for us who are believing," and so on, to the end of the chapter, a wonderful outpouring of prayer to follow the earlier outpouring of praise. PRAISE and PRAYER. The two ever go together. Truly we can laud our heavenly Father for all the vast riches with which He has blessed us, but we should never fail to add our supplications for a spirit of wisdom and revelation in the realization of Him—a spirit that will enable us to grasp, in some measure at least, the immense value of the treasures that are ours.

Now this wonderful first chapter of Ephesians opens with two peculiar phrases. We say peculiar because of the way they are used. The first is the expression "among the celestials" (*en tois epouraniois*). This occurs five times in the book of Ephesians, but nowhere else in the whole of Scripture. In contrast to this, we have a second phrase, "disruption of [the] world" (*katabolê kosmou*), which occurs altogether ten times in the Greek Scriptures, but only this once in the whole of the writings of Paul. So here, then, we have a peculiar situation— the use of two expressions, one of which is the special property of the Ephesian letter, a treasure not to be found outside of our treasure chest, while the other is, in the main, the property of Scriptures outside of the Pauline writings, but used just this once by Paul for a special reason. Whatever is to be understood by the disruption of the world (and we will return to this presently), the only reason why Paul introduces it into his Ephesian epistle is to place the origin of the ecclesia before it. We are chosen in Christ "*before* the disruption of the world," and the spiritual blessings that we receive are in accord with this fact.

AMONG THE CELESTIALS

The first of our two phrases establishes the setting for all that follows. We are no longer to regard the heavens as something distant and unattainable, but the Ephesian epistle places us right in the very midst of the heavens. The Concordant rendering, "among the celestials," gives the phrase a distinctive character, which is in keeping with its use in this epistle. We are to see ourselves as being in the heavens, surrounded by celestial hosts, just as the earth itself is a sphere in the midst of a universe of heavenly bodies. As Paul puts it in Philippians 3:20, "Our realm is inherent in the heavens"—that is to say, it *belongs there*. Cephas was *inherently* a Jew—he had never been anything else, and could not be anything else (Gal. 2:14). The man at the gate of the temple was *inherently* lame from birth—he had never known any other condition (Acts 3:2). Our realm is *inherent* in the heavens—it has never been anywhere else; in the sight of God, the ecclesia, which is the body of Christ, has always enjoyed celestial status; even while its members are sojourning in temporary tabernacles of flesh, its celestial citizenship has never been in doubt. That is why there is nothing at all out of place in our being blessed "with every spiritual blessing among the celestials." The blessings are appropriate to our state and to our status.

These lines are being written in England. If we in England were offered something in Australia, we might not appreciate it, and look rather askance at the giver. What use would it be to us here? In a wider field, if we, as mere citizens of earth, were offered spiritual blessings among the celestials, they would be even more useless, for we would have no means of attaining to them. They would be beyond our reach. But as citizens of the heavens, from the time that we were chosen in Christ before the disruption of the world, they are entirely appropriate, for they can be appreciated and enjoyed. Our treasures are worth having!

BEFORE THE DISRUPTION OF THE WORLD

It is in accord with the fact that we, the ecclesia, are chosen in Christ before the disruption of the world that we have this celestial status and these celestial blessings, because before the disruption of the world there was no human in existence. Adam was not created until after the disruption.

What, then, was the disruption? Let us remind ourselves that the disruption of the world is that event which occurred at the end of the first eon, when the earth became waste and barren, and darkness covered the face of the deep. In the Authorized (King James) Version, the word in Ephesians 1:4 is "foundation," but this is a mistranslation. The Greek word is *katabolê*. *Kata* means "down"; it comes through into English in such words as "cataclysm" and "catastrophe." *Bolê* means "casting" or "throwing." The whole means "down-casting"; in fact, the whole expression is brought through into English in the word "catabolism," which the dictionary defines as "the breaking down of complex bodies." By no stretch of imagination can we bring into it the thought of "foundation," yet this is what the translators of the Authorized Version have regretably done.

Here in Ephesians it is the *casting down*, the *disruption*, of the world that is being spoken of; and let it be noted that it is the casting down, or disruption, of the *world*, not of the earth. The world is the *kosmos*, or order of things, at that time; the society which included the heavens as well as the earth. Yes, there was a disruption of the heavens too. How do we know? Well, if there had been no disruption of the heavens—if they were still in their state of pristine purity—there would be no need for a new heavens as well as a new earth. Yet prophecy on this point is quite clear (Isa. 65:17; Rev. 21:1).

In earlier studies in this series, we have been stressing the point that the first rebellion against God was among His original creatures, those in the celestial realms before humanity was created. This rebellion could only have been against the headship and authority of the One Whom God had purposed to be first—the Son of His love. This rebellion brought about a disruption of the celestial society of that time, with the consequent establishment of sovereignties and authorities and powers and

lordships. Though these would originally be ordained
of God, they must, by their very nature, and like their
later earthly counterparts, move into a state of antagonism to God, Who wills to vest all sovereignty in His
own Son. Hence the need for the future administration
of the complement of the eras to restore the position by
heading up all in the Christ. But for this to happen
Christ Himself must first be exalted to a position which
is high above all others, and we find that this is what
actually occurs.

HEAD OVER ALL

Christ had emptied Himself of all His former glory
in order to descend to the depths of the cross; now, as
we read in verse 21 of Ephesians one, He is roused from
among the dead by the might of God's strength, and
seated at God's right hand, "up over every sovereignty
and authority and power and lordship, and every name
that is named, not only in this eon but also in that which
is impending." And now we find another wonderful
treasure in our chest, namely, that it is as "Head over
all" that God gives Him "to the ecclesia which is His
body, the complement by which all in all is being completed."

Yes indeed, Christ is already established as "Head
over all"; in all three prison letters this is clearly stated.
Philippians only confirms Ephesians when it says that
"God highly exalts Him, and graces Him with the name
that is above every name, that in the name of Jesus
every knee should be bowing, celestial and terrestrial and
subterranean, and every tongue should be acclaiming
that Jesus Christ is Lord, for the glory of God, the
Father" (Phil. 2:9-11). Colossians adds its confirmation when it states, in relation to all powers in heaven
and earth, whether visible or invisible, that they are all
"created through Him and for Him, and He is before
all, and all has its cohesion in Him; and He is the Head

of the body, the ecclesia, Who is Sovereign, Firstborn
from among the dead, that in all He may be becoming
first'' (Col. 1:16-19).

But if Christ is now exalted, it must follow that the
ecclesia, which is His body, shares His exaltation, for
our lot is cast in Him (Eph. 1:11). Colossians puts it
slightly differently, "Your life is hid together with
Christ in God." And then Paul adds, "Whenever Christ,
our Life, should be manifested, then you also shall be
manifested together with Him in glory." Is not this
wonderful? Christ cannot appear, cannot be manifested,
unless and until the ecclesia is with Him to be manifested
together with Him in glory. That is why the whole creation is groaning and travailing together until now (Rom.
8:22). It is waiting for the manifestation of the sons
of God. The ecclesia and Christ cannot function sepa-
rately; they must appear together and be seen to be
together and to function together. That is why we shall
always be "together with the Lord." And that is why,
in the second chapter of Ephesians, the ecclesia is portrayed as being seated together "among the celestials,
in Christ Jesus, that in the oncoming eons, He [God]
should be displaying the transcendent riches of His grace
in His kindness to us in Christ Jesus." Yet another
treasure in our treasure chest!

The ecclesia is the complement of Christ, just as woman
is the complement of man. There is an analogy here.
When a complement (AV: helpmeet) was to be provided
for man (Adam), it could not be found among all the
animal creation that was paraded before him (see Gen.
2:18-20). No, the complement must come from within.
Up to the time of the deep sleep falling upon Adam, his
complement had resided latent within himself, but on
awaking from his sleep and seeing the woman, Adam was
immediately aware of what had taken place, for he said,

"This was once bone of my bones and flesh from my flesh. This shall be called woman, for from her man is this taken" (Gen. 2:23).

The scripture in Genesis then proceeds to give the definition of marriage, and this is quoted by Paul, in Ephesians 5:31 as an illustration of the relationship between Christ and His ecclesia. Let us make it clear that the ecclesia is *not* the bride of Christ, for Adam never had a bride. A bride is always sought from without; Adam received his wife from within — she was his own flesh. Similarly, Christ does not seek His ecclesia which is His body, from without, for the scripture in Ephesians 1:4 makes it clear that it was chosen *in Him* before the disruption of· the world. Until God's Son fell into the deep sleep of death, the ecclesia lay dormant in Him, unseen and unheard of all down the time covered by the Hebrew Scriptures. But from the moment that Christ is roused from among the dead, the ecclesia (in the sight of God) becomes a separate entity, and will in due course be presented to Christ as "a glorious ecclesia, not having spot or wrinkle or any such things, but that it may be holy and flawless" (Eph. 5:27).

No illustration must be carried too far—never beyond what it is intended to illustrate. By the very nature of things, the woman must be presented to man as a complete being, and the ecclesia will be presented to Christ as a complete ecclesia. But there is no place in the illustration for the gradual process by which the ecclesia is called, one by one, from many generations of humanity spread over nearly two thousand years, nor for the fact that Christ presents the ecclesia to *Himself*.

But the illustration does support the truth that, once a complement is formed, the one from whom the complement is taken cannot fulfill its function in the purpose of God except through the complement. The former becomes the *means* by which God's operations are carried forward; the latter the *medium* through which they are

carried forward.   Man could obey the command of
Genesis 1:28 to "be fruitful and increase and fill the
earth, and subdue it" only through the woman who is
his complement.   Similarly, God has so designed His
purpose that Christ can fulfill His function of subjecting
and reconciling all to God only through the ecclesia which
is His body, *the complement by which all in all is being
completed* (or more literally: the complement of the
[One] completing the all in all, Eph. 1:23).

This is why Christ is at present regarded as being
seated at God's right hand; this is why His present
operations are scripturally defined as being on behalf of
His ecclesia (see Rom. 8:34; Eph. 5:25-27).   This is
why His future (and we trust, imminent) coming for
His ecclesia is so important: it is the event that will trig-
ger off a fresh impetus to God's purpose, leading to the
freeing of creation from the slavery of corruption (Rom.
8:21), and to all the events of 1 Corinthians 15:25-28.

WHY WE WERE CHILDREN OF INDIGNATION

It is at this point of our considerations that there
seems to be a tremendous difference between Christ and
His ecclesia.   Christ is completely without sin; the ecclesia is made up of sinners.   Or is it?   Is it made up of
sinners?   No, on the contrary, it is made up of righteous
ones.   In the Ephesian concept of the complement of a
sinless Christ, the ecclesia cannot be something that is
contaminated with sin; it must be holy and flawless.   By
the time we come to its position as it appears in the
Ephesian epistle, its members have passed through all
the stages of the Roman epistle.   We have been justified;
we have been made righteous in God's sight; nothing now
is condemnation to us in Christ Jesus.   But we were *once*
sinners; *once* we walked in accord with the eon of this
world; *once* we were in our nature children of indignation, even as the rest; but *now* we bask in the vast love
of God Who vivifies us together in Christ.   But if we

were chosen in Christ before the disruption of the world
and are therefore not in any way the offspring of rebellion, why are we called upon to pass through the experiences and tribulations of sinners?

There is more than one answer to this question, but in
the context of the Ephesian epistle that we are considering, the answer is that God needed those who had been
saved in grace in order to be able to display His grace
among the rebel celestial inhabitants of His universe. He
displays His grace to them by the way that He has dealt
with us. In our former state we were a pretty bad lot
like the rest of humanity, and the celestials, looking down
on humanity as a whole with all its depravity and violence, must be really appalled at what they see. But
then they see the ecclesia—the called-out ones, for that is
what the word "ecclesia" means—they see them declared
to be righteous and enjoying the favors of God, and they
will come to see that the grace, which the loving kindness
of God has showered upon us, is for them too. And what
is stated to be the present lot of the ecclesia in verses
8-10 of Ephesians 2, will be their lot also when they like-
wise become recipients of the grace of God.

THE RICHES OF GOD'S GRACE AND GLORY

These verses (8-10) give the ultimate in salvation,
when all creature endeavor is cast on one side and all is
found to be of God. "In grace, through faith, are you
saved, and this is not out of you; it is God's approach
present, not of works lest anyone should be boasting.
For His achievement are we, being created in Christ
Jesus for good works, which God makes ready beforehand, that we should be walking in them."

Yes, the transcendent riches of God's grace are to be
displayed among the celestials; but, as we saw earlier,
the influence of God's operations through the ecclesia
does not stop with the lesser lights among them. No,
indeed, far from it, for in the third chapter we find that

the multifarious wisdom of God is to be made known to the sovereignties and authorities among the celestials, through the ecclesia. And this, as again we noted earlier, is in accord with the purpose of the eons. This is what God's purpose is all about—the universal display of His grace and the ultimate reconciliation of all to Himself. This is what the ecclesia was created for. This is the calling with which we were called. It is nothing less than being the complement of Christ to bring God's purpose to its grand and glorious ultimate at the consummation of the eons.

In the prayer in the first chapter of Ephesians, Paul prays that we may perceive, among other things, what are the riches of the glory of the enjoyment of God's allotment among the saints. Notice this phrase carefully; it is another treasure in our chest. It is not our allotment, but God's, that is being referred to. Our allotment is in Christ; but God has an allotment among the saints. What is God's allotment? Why, it is just this, that the ecclesia is a vital feature in God's purpose. It is *through* the ecclesia that the word of the cross is proclaimed; it is *in* the ecclesia that the grace of God is seen. God has a tremendous allotment in the saints. If the cross of Christ is the hub of the wheel, then the saints are the spokes that radiate from the center.

But in that prayer of Ephesians 1, there is a remarkable phrase which we should note particularly. "The eyes of your heart having been enlightened." Not, "your eyes having been enlightened, that you may perceive," but "the eyes of your HEART having been enlightened."

The Authorized (King James) Version renders this phrase, "the eyes of your understanding being enlightened," and this would seem to take its application away from the heart and transfer it to the head—to the mind. The English Revised Version, Rotherham and Moffatt all use the word "heart," so does Weymouth in a footnote, and so, of course, does the Concordant Version. For the Greek word is *kardia*, and every medical student knows that a cardiac condition has to do with the heart and not with the head. We need an illuminated heart to be able to grasp and enjoy the blessings of the Ephesian epistle.

In the second prayer of Paul, in chapter 3, the point is carried a stage further, for here the apostle prays that Christ should "dwell in your hearts [not in your heads] through faith, that you, having been rooted and grounded in love, should be strong to grasp, together with all the saints, what is its breadth and length and depth and height—to know besides the knowledge transcending love of Christ—that you may be completed for the entire complement of God."

What a beautiful phrase is this, "having been rooted and grounded in love." Does this apply to you? Of course it does! It applies to all the members of the ecclesia. The whole ecclesia has been rooted and grounded in the love of God. It was in love that He designated us beforehand for the place of a son in Him. It is because of the vast love with which He loves us that we are vivified together in Christ. Yes, the foundations of the ecclesia are firm indeed—rooted and grounded in the vastness of God's love. And we, as individual members of the ecclesia, should be strong to grasp this fact with all its implications—its breadth and length and depth and height—and to know, besides, the knowledge transcending love of Christ, that we may be completely fitted out for the purpose for which God has chosen us.

THE SECOND KEY

We cannot be completed for the entire complement of God, and we cannot walk worthily of the calling with which we are called, unless the evangel of the grace of God has entered our hearts as well as our heads. That is why the whole of the second half of Ephesians is devoted to deportment, or behavior. We can walk worthily of the calling with which we were called only if, with all humility and meekness, with patience, we bear with one another in love and endeavor to keep the unity of the spirit with the tie of peace.

Back in an earlier letter of Paul (Rom. 5:5) we read that "the love of God is being poured out in our hearts through the holy Spirit which is being given to us." And here, in Ephesians 4:30, we are besought not to be giving sorrow to the holy Spirit of God by which we are sealed for the day of deliverance. And the way that we could cause sorrow to the holy Spirit of God is by allowing bitterness and malice to enter our hearts, and by saying unkind things about one another, and by engaging in malicious gossip and silly tittle-tattle. It is a sound principle: if we hear good about another, repeat it if we like, but if we hear evil, keep it as far as possible to ourselves, for evil generally becomes exaggerated in the telling of it. Paul says, "Let all bitterness and fury and anger and clamor and calumny be taken away from you with all malice, yet become kind to one another, tenderly compassionate, dealing graciously among yourselves, according as God also, in Christ, deals graciously with you."

In the oncoming eons we are to be used of God to display His grace among the celestials. Ought we not to be conditioning ourselves, preparing ourselves, for that service by being gracious to those with whom we are now in contact? Ought we not to become, as far as lies in our power, imitators of God, as beloved children, and be walking in love, according as Christ also loves us? Should not this be our daily aim, for only thus can we walk worthily of that supreme calling with which we are called?

The same advice is given to us in Philippians and Colossians. In the second chapter of Philippians, Paul pleads, "If, then, there is any consolation in Christ, if any comfort of love, if any communion of spirit, if any compassion and pity, fill my joy full, that you may be mutually disposed, having mutual love, joined in soul, being disposed to one thing—nothing according with faction, nor yet according with vainglory—but with humility, deeming one another superior to one's self, not each noting that which is his own, but each that of the others also. For let this disposition be in you, which is in Christ Jesus also." And in Colossians, we are entreated to put off anger, fury, malice, calumny, obscenity, out of our mouths. We are not to lie to one another. Rather, we are to "put on, then, as God's chosen ones, holy and beloved, pitiful compassions, kindness, humility, meekness, patience, bearing with one another and dealing graciously among yourselves, if anyone should be having a complaint against any. According as the Lord also deals graciously with you, thus also you. Now over all these put on love, which is the tie of maturity. And let the peace of Christ be arbitrating in your hearts, for which you were called also in one body; and become thankful."

Only by following these entreaties of Paul can we be true—true to the spirit by which we are sealed—true to the calling with which we are called. Then, being true, in love we should be making all grow into Him, Who is the Head, Christ, for out of Him the entire body is making for the growth of itself, for the upbuilding of itself in love (Eph. 4:15, 16).

This will not be easy, because, almost alone of God's creations, the ecclesia in this special era of grace has its spiritual enemies, who are constantly poised to attack. It is a fact that those who most need the grace of God are the ones who are the most virulent in their opposition to it. We refer to the sovereignties and authorities among the celestials, for it is against them that we wrestle—"the spiritual forces of wickedness among the celestials" (Eph. 6:12). It is against them and the Adversary, who is always opposed to God's purpose wherever it is revealed (and it is being revealed in the ecclesia today), that we need the protective panoply of God—another treasure in our chest! We are given only one offensive weapon, and that is the sword of the spirit, which is the Word of God. In the hands of Jesus, it destroyed the power of the Adversary in person; in our hands it will be used to destroy the antagonism of his minions to the grace of God. In our hands, it becomes a weapon of conciliation, if that is not a contradiction in terms, for we can use it in the light of the preaching of the cross.

.   .   .

Reluctantly, we close down our chest for the moment with a last glance at its many treasures, and what priceless treasures they are! The love of God has become to the ecclesia "the vast love with which He loves us." The love of Christ has become "the knowledge transcending love of Christ." The grace of God is now "the riches of His grace," and, in the oncoming eons, will be "the transcendent riches of His grace." The power of God is now "the transcendent greatness of His power for us who are believing." And the ecclesia itself, which is the body of Christ, becomes "the complement by which all in all is being completed."

What, then, are we to say about the calling with which we are being called? In another epistle, Paul describes it as "a holy calling, not in accord with our acts" (which would immediately and permanently disqualify us), "but in accord with God's own purpose, and the grace which is given to us *before times eonian*" (2 Tim. 1:9). Yes, the ecclesia was in the purpose of God even before He created the eons, and its ministry will not be completed until the final consummation, when God is All in all.

So we close down the lid of the first half of our chest with the doxology (or hymn of praise to God) that comes at the end of the third chapter of Ephesians:

"Now to Him Who is able to do superexcessively above

all that we are requesting or apprehending, according to the power that is operating in us, to Him be glory in the ecclesia and in Christ Jesus for all the generations of the eon of the eons! Amen!"

And we close down the lid of the second half with the benediction (or blessing from God and the Lord Jesus Christ) that comes at the end of the sixth chapter:

"Peace be to the brethren, and love with faith, from God, the Father, and the Lord Jesus Christ. Grace be with all who are loving our Lord Jesus Christ in incorruption! Amen!"

May our love for the Lord Jesus Christ and our love for one another be unfeigned; then shall we indeed walk worthily of the calling wherewith we are called. Amen!

BEFORE THE DISRUPTION OF THE WORLD

Three features in God's purpose are described in His Word as dating from "before the disruption of the world," and they are interrelated.

They are:

1. The love of God for His Son (John 17:28).
2. God's foreknowledge of the sacrifice of Christ (1 Pet. 1:20).
3. God's choice of the ecclesia, in Christ (Eph. 1:4).

These three features are expanded in the prison letters of Paul.

Colossians deals with the love of God for His Son, here specifically termed "the Son of His love," by emphasizing that all is *for* Him, and that in all He is to be becoming first. In this we have the *motive* behind God's purpose, namely, the glorification of His Son, which finds its ultimate in the reconciling of all to Himself through Him.

Philippians stresses the immensity of the sacrifice of Christ, by showing how He first emptied Himself of all His pristine glory to take up the form of humanity, and then humbled Himself to become obedient unto death, *even* the death of the cross, on account of which ("wherefore") God highly exalts Him. The cross is the *means* by which reconciliation is effected.

Ephesians associates the ecclesia with Christ, as His *complement*. The ecclesia is thus the *medium* through which reconciliation is to be completed.

THE ECCLESIA, WHICH IS HIS BODY

This ecclesia, which is the one specifically referred to in Paul's epistles, is presented to us in two distinct, yet related aspects. They are like the two sides of the same coin. From whichever side we look, we recognize the coin, yet the two aspects are different.

Individually, the ecclesia is composed of many members, each of which is foreknown, designated beforehand, called, justified and glorified (Rom. 8:28-30). Each is brought *into* Christ through baptism *into* His death (Rom. 6:3). Each is essential to the rest, and has his, or her, individual part to play in the upbuilding of the whole (1 Cor. 12:12-31; Eph. 4:11-14).

Collectively, the ecclesia is a unified body, chosen *in* Christ from before the disruption of the world, and seen by God as holy and flawless, its realm being inherent in the heavens and its service among the celestials. As such, it is the complement of Christ by which all in all is being completed.

It is in the individual aspect that members of the ecclesia were once sinners, all being by nature children of indignation even as the rest. This is changed when they come into Christ, for then they are "a new creation" (2 Cor. 5:17). But collectively, the ecclesia is always seen by God as being holy and flawless, for it was conceived in His purpose before the disruption which is the evidence of rebellion in the universe, and becomes a separate entity only after the question of sin has been settled once and for all on the cross.